CONTAINING CRISIS

A Guide to Managing School Emergencies

CONTAINING CRISIS
A Guide to Managing School Emergencies

Robert S. Watson, Ph.D.
Janice H. Poda, Ph.D.
C. Thomas Miller, Ed.D.
Eleanor S. Rice
Gary West

NATIONAL EDUCATIONAL SERVICE
Bloomington, Indiana   1990

Copyright © 1990 by National Educational Service

All rights reserved, including the right of reproduction of this book in whole or in part or in any form.

Edited by Ronald D. Stephens
Executive Director
National School Safety Center
Encino, California

recycled paper

Cover Design by Bryan Thatcher

Printed in the United States of America

LB
2864.5
.C66
1990

Table of Contents

Introduction vii

1 Everyday Planning.................................. 3
2 Preparing for School Emergencies 14
3 Making Decisions During an Emergency 18
4 Using Technology to Meet Communications Needs
    During an Emergency 24
5 Dealing with the Media During an Emergency 32
6 Dealing with Rumors During an Emergency 40
7 Managing Parent Reactions 43
8 Counseling and Other Continuing Service 47
9 Managing Public Relations Following an Emergency 52
10 Developing School Safety and Emergency Plans 57
11 Developing District Intervention and Emergency
    Management Plans........................... 64
12 Developing Staff Training and Inservice Activities....... 73
13 School Safety as a Function of School Design 77
APPENDIX A A Sample School Emergency/Safety Plan...... 83
APPENDIX B A Sample District Emergency Plan............ 99

Introduction

FEW things are as dramatic as a story of school children hurt or killed in an accident or an act of violence. Despite the headlines that sensationalize the stories, there is a great need for level-headed planning and action in the face of emergencies that endanger school children.

Parents are beginning to understand that such things do not just happen to other children—such things can happen to their children. Those parents are demanding that schools protect their children; they are also demanding to know what schools plan to do when an emergency occurs.

District and school personnel are being called upon to provide a safe and secure environment in which teachers can teach and students can learn. In addition, district and school staff must plan for management of events that cannot be predicted or prevented.

The events that led to the writing of this book covered a five-month period of 1988 in which two distinctly different types of tragedy threatened—and took—the lives of students and teachers in one school district.

This book, however, is not about one school district. It is not about the students, teachers, parents, or administrators in one school district. This book is not a simple listing of all the major school tragedies from the last five years (you can find such lists—under bold headlines—in any of a number of non-educational publications).

This book is about taking care of people when they need it most. This book is about answers to questions being asked in every community in this country.

This book is about learning—the hard way.

In 1988, Greenwood School District 50 in Greenwood, South Carolina, experienced two major tragedies that placed students and teachers in life-threatening situations. The first involved a chartered bus that overturned on an interstate highway while returning 47 students and teachers from a field trip. The second involved an armed intruder who shot several students and teachers, killing two third-graders.

The combined lessons learned form the basis of this book. The first-hand experiences of district and school staff provide real insights into the management of emergencies-in-the-making. We have talked with educators in other districts where students and teachers were involved in accidents and acts of violence. We have incorporated their suggestions and reactions, as well.

The following accounts of the emergencies faced by Greenwood School District 50 are provided for background. Many of the suggested plans and action were developed as a result of experiences dealing with those emergencies. Those experiences are used occasionally throughout the book to illustrate specific points.

An Off-Campus Emergency

On April 19, 1988, Greenwood School District 50 and the entire community of Greenwood, South Carolina were stunned to learn that a chartered bus with fourth-grade students from Pinecrest Elementary School had been involved in an accident approximately one hundred miles from Greenwood. The students were returning from a field trip to Charlotte, North Carolina. The phone call from the Emergency Preparedness Center at 4:30 P.M. informed the district superintendent that the bus had overturned on an interstate highway and that students, teachers, and parent chaperones had been injured — some seriously.

The bus that overturned was the last in a three-bus convoy returning to Greenwood. The driver of the second bus saw the third bus overturn and stopped to help. The first bus in the convoy was unaware of the accident and continued on its way. It would arrive in Greenwood almost two hours later — still unaware of the accident.

Rescue workers arrived within minutes and began the difficult task of determining the most critically injured and transporting the injured to area hospitals. Most of the student passengers had no form of identification with them; the adults who were capable of identifying students were also injured and unable to assist in that identification.

Since the principal was in San Francisco, attending a national conference, the superintendent was notified of the accident, and the search began immediately for information. It was known that almost all fourth-graders had gone on the trip. A list of students who had gone was kept at the school; however, there was no list of students assigned to each bus. In fact, four classes of fourth-graders were spread through the three buses. Waiting parents did not know whether their children were on the overturned bus, the bus that stopped to offer assistance, or the bus that was continuing on the return trip.

They also did not know where their children were being treated, since the injured were taken to the Piedmont Medical Center in Rock Hill, to the Chester County Hospital, and to Charlotte Memorial Hospital. These hospitals were as much as seventy miles apart.

Calls were made to the York County Emergency Preparedness Center, the South Carolina Highway Patrol, the three hospitals, and employees of the Rock Hill School District. It was difficult for officials from those agencies to know to whom they could release information because they did not know Greenwood 50 personnel. It was also difficult for officials to respond to requests for information because of the magnitude of the accident and the number of calls they received.

A teacher from the second bus, who had helped with the injured children at the accident scene, confirmed the patients' names at Piedmont Medical Center. Those names were compared to the class lists from the school's computer database. Through that process, the most seriously injured patients at Charlotte Memorial Hospital were identified. School district personnel located the parents and the spouses of the injured. Some parents and spouses were instructed to phone the hospital to give permission for treatment.

Other major problems included sketchy information, jammed phone lines, and rumors.

An On-Campus Emergency

About five months later, another major emergency involved students and teachers in the same school district. On September 26, 1988, Oakland Elementary School was the scene of the worst possible school crisis. A man entered the school building through the front door, walked into the cafeteria while first-graders were eating lunch, and started shooting, wounding three students and one teacher. He left the cafeteria, reloaded his hand gun, and entered a third-grade classroom where he again emptied the gun at students. One third-grade student died in the school and another died three days later. In addition to the two deaths, two teachers and seven students were wounded during the shooting.

The gunman had parked in the parking area in front of the school, waved to the custodian who was working in the school yard, and walked past the open door to the school's offices. He entered the cafeteria, where teachers always sat at the table nearest the door. He shot the first teacher who questioned his being there. He then emptied the gun at students and other teachers.

When he left the cafeteria, he went into a restroom and reloaded his gun. He shot the teacher who had followed him from the cafeteria and who had tried to keep him in the restroom. He then went into a third-grade classroom, where he again emptied his gun at students.

The violence took so little time that some classes were still in progress in parts of the building while students were escaping through classroom windows in other parts of the building. As the sense of emergency spread, the building emptied, with students running into nearby woods, across streets into neighborhood yards, and anywhere else that seemed to offer safety.

Within minutes, the gunman, who had dropped his gun in the third-grade classroom, was captured by school personnel. School personnel notified law enforcement agencies, emergency medical services, and district personnel. Some school personnel provided care for those who had been shot, while others began the task of finding and accounting for all the students who had run from the building. Teachers formed student groups on the front lawn so parents could find them. Less than two hours after the shooting began, all students had gone home except those who had been taken to the hospital for treatment.

On the day after the shooting, students were instructed to stay home while teachers and other school staff began to deal with the realities of the situation. Teachers would not eat in the cafeteria where the shooting started. They were confused and horrified. They did not feel safe. They were not ready to help students feel safe.

Parents were angry and frustrated. They questioned the school's inability to protect their children. They questioned the school and district administrators about safety and security. They did not feel that the school would be safe for their children.

Months later, the gunman came to trial. Students, teachers, and school administrators re-told their stories. The re-telling brought back fears and nightmares for children and adults. The appeals process could continue through 1995.

Other Situations

Other recent school emergencies include shootings in Winnetka, Illinois; Stockton, California; Lakeland, Florida; Washington, D.C.; and a hostage-taking in Montgomery, Alabama. Students in a kindergarten class were forced to witness a brutal assault on their teacher. A drunken driver killed children and adults returning from a church-related activity. A distressed student shot fellow students in response to the news that his family was planning to move to another state. A junior high school teacher photographed and filmed students in pornographic acts and shared the photos and film through a nationwide network of child pornographers. A non-custodial parent kidnapped a student from school because school personnel did not know the parent should not have the child.

In addition to the acts of direct violence toward students and staff in schools, other types of emergencies must be managed by school officials. Those might include earthquakes (the Bay Area was fortunate that the 1989 earthquake happened after schools were out for the day), tornadoes, high winds (which caused the wall of a school cafeteria to fall into a room full of children in 1989), flash floods, suicides, accidental deaths of students and staff, gang violence, rioting in school or at an athletic event, or chemical spills at nearby industries.

The Purpose for Writing This Book

School emergencies are chaotic situations born out of natural or man-made disasters or from willful violence. School emergencies can be small and easily managed or they can be large and difficult to manage. Every school emergency, however—large or small—*must* be managed in a way that ensures the safety of all those involved.

A school emergency has an immediate and powerful impact on the school, the district, the families of students and staff, and the local and extended communities. Appropriate management on the part of school authorities and community leaders can provide for the anticipated needs of those involved and can reduce or eliminate unanticipated negative consequences.

When emergencies occur, school personnel can be thrust into life-threatening situations which demand logical, rational, and responsible action. Experience in handling past emergencies is good preparation for administrators; however, most school administrators do not have such experience. For this reason, planning and training for the management of school emergencies are important. Personnel who know what to do in a disaster and who can function according to a prearranged plan can substantially contribute to successful crisis management.

This book discusses school emergencies — in their diversities and their commonalities — and makes recommendations that may help school administrators prepare, respond, and contain a crisis.

Who Should Read This Book

The book has been written for school administrators, teachers, district administrators and staff, and for district policymakers, such as the members of the boards of education. It is only through their concerted efforts that critical needs can be met to ensure the safety and well-being of all students during an emergency.

How to Use This Book

This practical training guide is based on the collective experiences of school and district administrators, faculty, and staff. The recommendations grow out of specific circumstances school officials had to face.

Thirteen chapters, separated roughly into five major topic areas, compose this book. Chapters 1 and 2 include information that will be needed as school and district personnel begin planning for the management of school emergencies. Chapters 3 through 7 include insights into the problems encountered during the management of school emergencies. Chapters 8 and 9 focus on information and needs that continue after the emergency is over. Chapters 10 through 13 outline the steps necessary to develop school and district emergency plans. The appendices provide reference materials that can be used in the planning process.

Conclusions

Despite significant differences in the major emergencies that have occurred in schools throughout the United States, many common factors suggest specific planning, preparation, and response strategies. Schools plan and prepare for the management of the immediate crisis and the continuing crisis aftermath.

Planning with insight is much easier than planning with hindsight.

CONTAINING CRISIS
A Guide to Managing School Emergencies

1
Everyday Planning

A SCHOOL'S OPERATION involves many tasks that are not directly related to life-threatening situations. In emergency situations, however, those functions and tasks take on special significance. This chapter examines those functions and tasks in relation to potential needs in emergency situations.

Learning in the School Setting

Parents send their children to school for many reasons. Most of those reasons relate to education and the desire that children learn to live in their changing environment.

School staff and administrators are conscientious and caring people. These are typical traits, even seeming to be prerequisites for teaching and supporting the teaching process. Educators live by the often-unstated axiom that students can learn from the experiences and knowledge of others and that such learning can benefit the lives of those students. Educators plan for positive learning experiences and deliver the appropriate activities to the students who leave the relative safety of their homes to come into the more public setting of a school campus.

As students leave their homes each morning, the school has responsibility for everything that happens to them until they return home that same day.

The school, then, must provide an environment in which students can take advantage of the available learning opportunities. When a crisis occurs during the school day, however, educators may find themselves in a learning situation for which no specific activities have been planned. In those circumstances, the time taken to learn can be critical. For that reason, educators must learn as much as possible *before* circumstances require them to learn. Learning from the knowledge and experience of others is preferable to learning during a school crisis. Planning for the management of such crises is a natural next step to that learning process.

Planning for Problems

Schools already know how to plan for potential problems. For example, many schools have procedures for picking up students on stranded buses, for contacting parents of those injured in school activities, for releasing students to adults who come for them, for bomb threats, for student violence, for students with infectious diseases, for weather-related emergencies, and the many other anticipated crises.

Most schools have procedures by which students can legitimately be in the halls during scheduled class time. Those procedures usually involve a hall pass, issued by the teacher who has current responsibility for the student. When the student returns to the class, he or she must show a signature of an adult who accepted responsibility for the student when he or she arrived at the stated destination. A great deal of effort goes into the planning and implementation of such a system of student accountability — especially when there is a violation of the procedure.

Similarly, strict guidelines ensure that monies collected by teachers are receipted and turned in to the appropriate school official within a reasonable amount of time. Often, when those guidelines are not followed, much energy goes into correcting the situation, whether that involves reprimanding or re-training those who are in error.

In recent years, there appear to have been fewer school fires than there have been acts of violence or other school emergencies. Most schools have regular fire drills (and students understand what to do in the event of fires or other events that require evacuation of the building). Yet schools typically do not have crisis drills and procedures for reacting to other events, such as intruders or student violence.

There are several reasons for that. Many school administrators and staff members believe that such things simply will not happen at their schools. Many school and district administrators feel that enough effort and energy have gone into planning for those things that can be anticipated and for those things that are required by local ordinances. Furthermore, many officials feel that the monies required for planning, training, and equipping for events that probably will not take place could be spent more effectively for instructional materials. Such confidence, however, is not justified. In fact, school crime and violence are increasing.

While the vast majority of events on school campuses prove to be positive learning experiences, schools nationwide have more than their share of problems. Each year, nearly three million incidents of school crime and violence occur. These are not merely disciplinary arguments; they are criminal acts such as assault, theft, and vandalism.

It is impossible to anticipate and prepare for the management of many events. When those events can be anticipated, it may be impossible to prevent their happening. In a school emergency, though, there is little time to plan additional procedures for managing students, staff, and other factors. With that in mind, school administrators and staff must understand that the successful management of some events may hinge on existing policies, procedures, and guidelines — although they were not planned and implemented with those specific events in mind.

Within a school's everyday operation, various types of information are collected and filed, various guidelines are planned and posted, and various procedures promote the smooth operation of the school. With appropriate attention to existing policies, procedures, and guidelines, school can develop foundations from which successful management of emergencies can arise.

Student and Staff Records

Schools must keep records. Complete and accurate student records are key components in the successful management of a school emergency. More importantly, student records may provide critical information in saving the life of a student.

Parents should be encouraged to provide accurate, updated information. In addition to directory information (address, telephone number, parents' names, work phone numbers, etc.), student records should include significant medical data such as allergic reactions, current medication, and restrictions on blood transfusions. In addition, conditions that might cause behavior changes — such as epilepsy, brain tumors, or emotional and psychological disorders — must be part of a student's record. All records should be clearly marked to indicate such factors — without requiring a search through those records.

Computerized Student Databases

The simplest use of a computer and software in school management is the creation and maintenance of a student database. The database can contain information about students, such as full names, addresses, phone numbers, medical needs and considerations, and class schedules. Some schools also keep discipline records, attendance, and grades in their student files.

In effect, computer-based student information can include much of the data kept in paper files. The advantage of computer-based files is that the data can be more easily and quickly retrieved than from paper files.

All schools keep some type of student medical information. This includes information about allergies, blood type, and the child's specific medical needs. School records should also include information that might influence medical treatment, such as religious beliefs, current medication, and existing conditions (such as epilepsy or diabetes).

Whether using a paper-based system or a computer-based system, many schools do not keep current or accurate information on their staff. Immediately following the shooting at Oakland Elementary School, computer records were used to get phone numbers and addresses of the students who had been shot. Those computer records also contained staff data; however, the staff records had not been given a high priority. The school was unable to find a telephone number or an address for the spouse of the most critically injured teacher. It is important that the school maintain records for everyone who works in the building.

Two pieces of information that should be prominent in all students' records involve transportation to and from school. The first piece of information is the manner in which a student travels to and from school. The second piece of information is a list of persons the parents have approved for picking up the student during the school day (or after school, if the regular transportation changes).

A computerized student database can include the bus number and route for each child who rides a school bus. In case of an accident, the computer can be used to print a list of students who were on the bus, a list of those who were delivered home on the route prior to the accident, a list of students who would not be on the bus because they were absent that day, and other information that might be needed for students who were involved in the accident. Without the computer, much more time would be required in gathering that type of information—delaying the delivery of needed services to students and parents.

Immediately following the bus accident involving students from Pinecrest Elementary School in Greenwood, South Carolina, the district's computer staff added data fields to the student database. Those fields were added in an effort to assist parents waiting at the school to find out the name of the hospital to which their children had been taken.

Fields for location and condition were added to the student screen. As calls came in from those hospitals (and as the children were identified), the information was added to each student's record. Lists were printed every few minutes and shared with those parents who were still waiting. That process permitted the collec- and distribution of information without the need for continuous checking for information already received.

A computer-based student and staff database can be an important tool in the daily operation of a school. It can also be an important tool in the management of a school emergency.

This can be done in a variety of ways. If the records are kept in a computer system, the factors can be flagged on-screen. If paper records are kept, the factors can be color-coded on the tab of the record folder.

Staff records should include any information that will permit adequate attention to their needs in times of emergencies, since staff members may be injured or may be required to take care of injured students.

In addition to directory information, staff records should note special skills and training. For example, a teacher who has had cardio-pulminary resuscitation (CPR) training may be able to save a student's or colleague's life—if someone in the building knows to call upon that teacher at the time of need.

Staff records should also indicate factors that might interfere with a teacher's ability to assist injured students. If a teacher cannot function in the midst of severe injury, the school administrators must be able to provide backup for that teacher in an emergency involving such injuries.

Early Dismissal of Students

Procedures for early student dismissal should be planned to ensure students' safety and to reassure parents, since early dismissal of a student is an opportunity for a non-custodial parent or other adult to get the student without parental permission.

Kidnapping has become an increasing concern of parents, and that concern must be addressed in school procedures. Kidnapping, however, is not the only possible abuse of early dismissal procedures. Students may, in fact, want to go with someone who comes for them. Someone posing as a relative may be there only to pick up a student who will then be involved in activities (drugs, sex, crimes, or others) at a time when the parents believe he or she is in school and when the school believes he or she is at home.

Student records should include the names of all adults authorized, by the parents, to pick up the child at school. Those names should include those who may come for early dismissal or for regular dismissal at the end of the school day.

Dismissal procedures should require that teachers not release a student from a classroom to anyone other than office staff. Office staff should not go to a classroom for a student until they have checked the student record for the name of the person who has come to pick up the student. If that person's name is not on the list or if that person cannot provide identification, the child should not be dismissed.

At the beginning of each school year, parents should be asked to indicate the normal manner in which their child will leave campus. At the end of each school day, every student should leave school by the normal means. The only exceptions would require a signed note from the parent or a visit by the parent, indicating that an exception is to be made for that day. In the case of notes, telephone confirmation is an excellent follow-up. Telephone calls from parents, however, without written confirmation, should not be accepted.

Parent and student orientation programs and printed guidelines should be part of the planning and implementation of the dismissal procedures. Parents and students will cooperate when they understand the reasons for those procedures—and those reasons always involve the safety and security of the students.

Access to the Building and Campus

Public access to school buildings and campuses is an issue that must be addressed during the everyday operation of a school. Parents must always be welcome and not locked out; students must always feel safe, yet not locked in.

Building and Classroom Security

Most existing school buildings are not designed and built with security in mind. Schools that are built in the future must be designed with safety and security in mind.

In the present, however, each building principal should assess the physical plant and decide which parts of the building are most vulnerable to safety and security problems. Steps can be taken to make every building safer—if the need for such safety is known.

One of the major problems in schools involves unauthorized persons entering the buildings. Locking all doors to keep those persons out is not practical or safe. At most schools, students can be found outside at all times of the school day. Recess, physical education classes, nature trails, and outdoor classrooms meet outside. If there is a threat to the safety of the students who are engaged in out-of-doors activities, precious time can be lost while someone is trying to unlock a door. A matter of minutes can mean the difference between life and death.

A school should be made as safe as possible; however, it should not become a prison for students and staff. It is a public building. People must be allowed to visit the school—in fact, people should want to visit schools.

Locking all doors to a school building sends signals to students and parents—it's not safe to be in the school. Parents who want to visit their children or who might volunteer to help in the school will not want to do so in an unsafe environment. The public perceptions of the school will be lowered.

Doors that are not used after classes begin can be locked from the outside, however. At Oakland Elementary School, one of the two front entrances and the door to the teachers' parking lot are locked at 8:30 each day. Those doors are not needed during the regular school day, and they are not located in areas where students or staff will need access to the building in an emergency. Other doors to the bus-loading area, to the playground areas, and to other outside areas through which students may move during the day are kept open. Locking a few doors from the outside does not violate fire codes if those in the building can leave through those doors simply by pushing a panic bar.

Most classroom doors have locks. Those are usually there to keep intruders out when no one is in the classroom. They require keys on both sides of the door. Schools should look at alternatives so those doors can be left unlocked during the instructional day but can be locked immediately in case of trouble. House locks, that require a key on the outside but have a twist button on the inside, would be ideal for classroom doors. In that way, a key will not be needed to lock the door from the inside, making it possible for teachers and their students to lock the doors after receiving word from the office that there is potential danger outside the classroom.

There should be some process by which all people entering the building are screened. Because of many entrances to buildings, screening all people can be difficult. Monitors would not attempt to prevent an intruder from going further; they would simply be an early-warning system that would alert the office of the intruder. In everyday operations, their main responsibility would be to direct visitors to the main office. Then the office personnel would deny or allow entrance to the rest of the building.

Campus and Playground Security

Most campuses have more than one traffic entrance. Because of building design, those entrances are sometimes hidden from the view of persons inside the building. During the day, barricades should be placed at the entrances that are used only at the beginning and at the end of the school day.

Those barricades can be nothing more than wooden sawhorses or pipes stood on end in holes drilled in the pavement. The purpose will be to keep unwanted traffic off the campus; however, such passive barricades are easily moved by anyone who really wants to drive onto the campus. Yet those barricades will force such drivers to leave their cars to move them, to drive over and through them, or to drive around them. All those actions should alert someone on campus, and they should alert the office whenever any vehicle enters the blocked drives.

Playgrounds should be as safe as classrooms—yet that is not totally possible. Playgrounds, simply by being outdoors, are harder to secure. Fences can help. If playgrounds are fenced, there should be gates in each side. In an emergency situation, students may be unable to return to the building. There should be more than one escape route.

Gates may be more than escape routes—they may also be the routes taken by intruders into the playground. As with the barricades, the gates and the entire fence line create a boundary of safety. When a stranger is observed entering the playground, an alert should go to the office and all students and teachers should return immediately to the building.

Communication between persons on the playground and the

school office is essential. Walkie-talkies can help meet those communication needs. At least one teacher on the playground should have a walkie-talkie that can reach the base station in the school office.

School procedures must include the positive identification of all school visitors. The school entrances should be designed to ensure that visitors are identified before they are permitted access to the student areas. While in the school, visitors should wear easily seen and clearly identifiable badges to indicate that they have permission to be in the building. School procedures must include the interception and removal of persons who do not follow those procedures.

All visitors, parents and others, should go directly to the school office upon arrival at the school. Appropriate signs directing visitors to the office should be strategically placed around the campus. The visitor should sign the daily visitors' log, and someone in the office must positively identify the visitor. If the visitor is allowed to visit in the building, he or she must wear the visitor's badge provided by the office. This badge identifies the visitor and lets all students and staff know that this visit has been cleared by the office personnel.

Staff and students must know the procedures for reporting persons who are not wearing the appropriate badge. Orientation programs for students, staff, parents, and other community members can be used to outline the procedures, the reasons for those procedures, and the consequences of not following them. The school staff—specifically, the office staff—must be consistent and diligent in following those procedures and requiring that all visitors follow them.

Communications

Communication is the key to both preventing and, if necessary, managing a school emergency. Some school campuses are quite large, making communication difficult between and among areas of the campuses. For this reason, the following are necessary:

• Adequate intercom or public address systems must exist and must function. A two-way communication system in every classroom is vital. Most intercom systems are adequate for communicating with classrooms from the office; however, the ability to initiate a call from a classroom to the office may save time and lives during an emergency.

• Walkie-talkies are effective tools for communicating with the office from various locations in the building or on the campus grounds. While students are on the playground, at least one teacher should have a walkie-talkie with which to communicate with the office. Office staff should know how to use the walkie-talkies and how to interpret communication coming from the playground (if codes are used to request assistance or report intruders).

Students should be trained to use the communication system. It is possible that an emergency incapacitates the teacher. There have been cases of the teachers choking, having heart attacks, or encountering other problems that will prevent or reduce their ability to contact the office.

Communication with the custodial staff is always important. In everyday operations, custodians are needed to deal with many kinds of emergencies—almost all of which are minor. Some schools will simply use the intercom system to page the custodians for such emergencies; some will use beepers. Those will serve the purpose of contacting the custodian wherever he or she may be on the campus.

Custodians, however, can do much more than answer paging systems as they assist with emergencies in schools.

Custodians move about the building and campus all during the school day. They are aware of more activity on the campus than anyone else. They can be a valuable resource in preventing and managing emergencies—if they can communicate with the office when they observe something that is suspicious.

All custodial staff should have walkie-talkies. If something out of the ordinary occurs, or if a stranger appears on the campus, they can notify the school office immediately.

Off-Campus Activities

Off-campus activities, including field trips, are important parts of every child's educational program. Safety procedures should be implemented before field trips are scheduled. In addition, measures should be taken to ensure the easiest means of managing an emergency—if one should occur during the off-campus activity.

Participating students should wear name tags that will not peel off or be easily removed. Sometimes name tags are stuck or pinned to coats or sweaters. If the coat or sweater is no longer needed, it may be taken off without regard for the name tag. This may be especially true if the vehicles in which the students are riding are heated enough to warrant removal of coats and sweaters. If an accident occurs, students may not be wearing the only means with which medical service persons can identify them.

Students should wear their identification tags at all times during the outing. Hospital-type bracelets can be used, particularly for younger children, because they will not come off easily.

Any time students are taken away from the campus, a route map and itinerary should be left at the school and that route should be followed for the trip. Students should leave and return to the school in the same vehicle, and rosters of the students in those vehicles should be left at the school before departure. Seating charts can be helpful, if they are available.

Conclusions

By maintaining appropriate information in student and staff records, by planning and implementing appropriate procedures and resources, schools can better manage unanticipated emergencies.

These are but a few of the many procedures that can be important in emergency management. It is hoped that these examples will prompt schools to look more closely at their current management procedures in order to expand their abilities to serve children in times of crisis.

2
Preparing for School Emergencies

ADVANCE PLANNING for the management of school emergencies includes the pre-assigned roles for school and district staff, communications, transportation, crowd control, and the involvement of local agencies that are prepared to assist in dealing with emergencies. This chapter includes—in general terms—the who, what, when, where, and why of advance planning. Following chapters will provide details of planning and management.

Who to Involve in Advance Planning

Planning for the management of school emergencies should involve district, school, and community representatives and resources. Each of those populations has resources that can be used in managing a school emergency.

It is logical to start the planning process at the school level. Teachers and other professional staff, paraprofessional staff, administrative and secretarial staff, custodial and maintenance staff, and food service staff should be represented on school-level planning committees. In addition, at least one district-level administrator should be included.

Police and sheriff departments, fire departments, emergency medical services, and the local emergency preparedness agencies should be included. Local businesses, especially those that are near the school and those that deal with hazardous chemicals or materials, should also be invited to the planning sessions.

Most importantly, invite parents to assist with the planning. Parents can provide a comprehensive background of concerns. They are aware of local resources and can help identify specific areas that need direct attention.

When plans exist for all schools in a district, a district-level team should be gathered from school staff, district staff, service agencies, and community members. That team will plan the coordination of the district's efforts with the specific needs of each school.

When the district plan is completed, it and the school plans should be reviewed by service agencies and community groups. Those agencies and groups should coordinate their action plans with those of the schools and district.

What to Involve in Advance Planning

Each school will have unique planning needs based on the facility layout, nearby industry, traffic patterns, communications capabilities, and other factors. A school plan must address those unique needs, possible emergency situations, and alternative courses of action for each possibility.

The first step in the planning process should be an examination of the building, campus, and immediate surroundings. A team of school staff and parents can assess those facilities and can make a report to the whole planning committee.

As those facilities are inspected, the team should look for evacuation routes and alternatives. If prior arrangements are made with churches and other meeting facilities, schools may be able to move large groups of students to those facilities at times with school buildings must be evacuated.

Student transportation must be considered by the planning group at a school. If a school must be closed early (as was the case following the shooting at Oakland Elementary School in Greenwood, South Carolina), there must be some plan for transporting students away from the school building. In addition—and more importantly—arrangements must be made for the safety of the children as they are delivered home. In many cases, there may be no one at home to let them in or to supervise them. Planning for such circumstances must involve communication with parents, previous understanding of the plan—by those parents and by their employers—and the total well-being of the children involved.

Planning must include in-service training. Both staff and students must know what to do during and immediately following an emergency. If students know, for example, when they evacuate a building in extreme situations that they are to go directly to a predefined location away from the school campus, school staff will have an easier time accounting for those students after the immediate crisis is under control.

Besides evacuation and transportation, planning groups should assess communications needs, classroom and playground activity, student checkout and pickup procedures, the safety of students riding school buses and the safety of students who walk to and from school, fire and tornado procedures, and other areas that may involve the safety of students in the school. Such an assessment for a school near an airport should certainly include takeoff and landing paths of aircraft.

Planning should address student safety in terms of visitor access. Parents must be willing to understand the need for visitor check-in and check-out procedures. Although such procedures can be troublesome for parents who want to visit their child's classroom, those procedures must ensure the safety of all students — including the students whose parents feel inconvenienced.

Procedures for bomb threats, intruders, student violence, and other campus crises must be addressed in the plan. Plans should also include assistance to service agencies that will be involved in the identification of students and staff.

Although it is difficult to anticipate school emergencies, it is very possible to plan for the most likely. From the assessment of school facilities and surroundings, the school planning committee can address the most plausible of events. In that planning, several action strategies can be recommended.

When to Begin and When to Continue Advance Planning

Advance planning should be done prior to the need for planning. That is not always the easiest time to plan, however. Many people will not see the need for immediate attention to safety problems and will not feel the urgency for action. Many will simply feel that school emergencies will never involve the students in their schools.

Advance planning should include regular and frequent review and revision of existing plans. Staff and circumstances change and existing plans must change in consideration of those.

Where to Begin Advance Planning

Schools should begin planning for safety first. That planning starts in the classroom, the playground, and the building; however, it must also include supervision for early arrivals and late leavers, early dismissals, people authorized to pick up students at school, and recognition of symptoms indicating personal problems — among many others.

When safety plans are in place, schools must then address crisis prevention. Procedures that ensure student supervision, visitor identification, and facility maintenance can prevent many school emergencies.

At the district level, planning should begin with intervention and management procedures. Immediately after an emergency occurs, district staff should come to the assistance of the school, providing assistance with all areas not directly related to the well-being of students and staff. If district staff manage the press, traffic, communications, and other necessary parts of the management process, school staff can deal directly with the needs of the students, staff, and parents.

The roles of all school staff should be defined with regard to their ability to contribute to management of the emergency.

Why Advance Planning Is Necessary

Advance planning is necessary because many children will be relying on relatively few adults for their well-being in time of crisis. Without advance planning, those adults are less likely to be able to serve the needs of the children. These are obvious reasons.

Another reason is based on an important axiom of law and common sense: knowledge leads to increased liability. School administrators know that violence directed toward schools and toward persons in schools is increasing. With that knowledge comes a responsibility for the increased safety needs of those schools and persons. With that responsibility comes increased liability whend the emergency management process is inadequate — or is perceived to be inadequate.

That does not mean that there is no liability in ignorance. In this age of information and information processing, school administrators certainly have a responsibility to know.

Conclusion

Advance planning should involve as many school, district, and community resources as possible. Plans should address the most likely events but should be flexible enough to ensure adaptability to unanticipated events.

3
Making Decisions During an Emergency

ESTABLISHING a command center, with ancillary information and decision centers, is an important part of the emergency management process. Consideration must be given to the needs of all groups involved in the emergency—students, teachers, administrators, parents, press, community members, and others. This chapter describes the establishment of such centers, including the tasks that must be managed from those centers. It also provides a discussion about setting up centers from which to manage a school emergency. The discussion can be viewed by the reader from two perspectives: (1) the discussion can be incorporated into advance planning for emergency management, or (2) the discussion can be a deadline for actually managing a school emergency. It is best to plan in advance; however, when such plans do not exist, the procedures presented in this chapter can serve as guidelines for management.

The information presented here cannot, and should not, substitute for local planning, training, and implementation of emergency management procedures.

The Command Center,
Information Centers, and Decision Centers

When a school emergency occurs, the public generally looks to the school for decisions and information. Other sites—particularly the district's administrative offices and the site of an off-campus accident—may be involved in information collection and decision-making; however, the school itself is the most logical location from which to disseminate information and decisions.

School administrators and staff must begin the immediate management process by securing the students' safety, analyzing the events, and contacting appropriate agencies for assistance. As the extent of the emergency is assessed, school administrators and staff must account for all students and colleagues. That process will not be easy or short, in most cases.

When district administrators and staff arrive at the school, school administrators and staff can continue their tasks of dealing with the immediate needs of students, staff, and others. District staff, then, begin the process of establishing a command center, collecting information to be shared with the public and the media, and establishing decision centers at other sites that will be involved in the emergency management process.

Identification of Injured Students and Staff

The first step in any emergency is identifying the injured. It is often difficult to immediately identify people who are injured or killed during an emergency. Many times the adult supervisors are injured to the extent that they are unable to assist with the identification of students.

The need to identify the injured immediately is necessary for several reasons. Obviously, parents and spouses must be notified immediately. In an emergency, medical treatment may be required and special consideration may be required for some persons with known allergies or preferences. Permission to provide treatment is often required, as well.

When possible, identification of the injured should be completed before the injured are removed from the campus; however, identification efforts should not interfere with the provision of medical services.

As the injured are identified, it will be helpful to list their names and condition. It will also be helpful to attach some identification to them prior to their being removed to medical facilities. That will help hospital staff find existing records and will help in directing family members to the appropriate doctors and areas of the hospital.

Freedom of Information regulations may prevent the school's release of names following an emergency. Some states restrict the identification of injured persons until the notification of family. In some states, schools cannot release the names of persons injured at a school; however, when those persons are place in an ambulance and taken to a hospital, their names become public information and the hospital may release those names without any delays.

If the emergency is off campus, the school remains the most logical place from which to gather and disseminate information.

If the school maintains an emergency kit, as described in

Appendix A, staff can find the tools necessary for identifying injured students and adults and for placing that identification on them before they are taken from the campus. Using a ballpoint pen to write names on the hands of the injured will save time and effort on the part of school staff, parents, and medical personnel. (Note that it is best to use ballpoint pens for this purpose. Felt-tip or other types of pens use washable inks that may be inadvertently removed in preparation for medical treatment.)

Parents of students who are not injured during a school emergency will have the same fears as the parents of those who are injured — until they are assured their children are safe.

For that reason, identifying uninjured students and staff is also an important function of the command center. Following the Pinecrest bus accident, there was a need for identifying the students who had been on the bus that stopped to help the injured. The adults on the second bus were busy in their immediate efforts to provide first aid and comfort. Later they were involved in identifying the injured students and adults. The uninjured were taken to a church until the adults could get back to them. At the school site, parents of those children had no way of knowing whether their students were involved in the accident or were at the church.

Following the shooting at Oakland, students were gathered from the nearby wooded areas and the neighborhood streets. Teachers had their gradebooks and class rosters and went about the process of accounting for their students. The principal's role was that of coordinator and follow-up strategist. If a teacher reported a missing student, the principal had to determine the status of that student, checking the name against lists of injured and dead.

In Stockton, California, teachers accounted for their students and the uninjured students were released to their parents, one class at a time in a planned location rather than having a chaotic, unorganized procedure where all the parents could march onto the campus.

Information Needs

In a school emergency, all kinds of information will be needed, such as telephone numbers and medical information which should be available in up-to-date and complete records on students and staff. There are also less obvious needs that cannot be anticipated. For example, immediately after the Oakland shooting, rumors began to fill the gaps where facts were not readily available. One of the strongest rumors was that the shooting was racially motivated —

the alleged gunman had been white and the two reported fatalities were black. Such a rumor, true or not, could have created additional emergencies within sections of most communities. The student records at Oakland included student pictures that were immediately placed on an easel so the press could use the information. Half of the wounded were white, the other half black. Without specifically addressing the rumor, the district and the school were able to avoid other crises that could have come from the shooting but which were not directly related to the shooting.

There were no photographs available, however, of the teachers who were shot. Personnel practices dictate that photographs not be part of the employment applications. Districts and schools might consider requesting photographs after hiring each employee, though. The photographs can be returned whenever the employee leaves the district.

Gathering information is a prime function of an emergency command center. Other centers may be established to gather specific pieces of information, as needed. For example, one or more district employees should be sent to the hospital to provide specific information to those at the school. Those at the hospital may also help parents who come to the hospital as their children are admitted.

As the district office staff manage the emergency, the superintendent becomes the major decision-maker. Information on which decisions are based may come from various sources. Someone from the district should be at each site from which that information is gathered. As the information is collected, it must be compiled and coordinated so it can be shared with parents, the press, and other groups.

Notification of Other Schools in the District

If an emergency situation evolves at one school in the district, other schools in that district will be affected. When a major emergency occurs at one school, parents will immediately begin picking up students at other schools. In order to assist those students and parents, other schools must have reliable and accurate information.

The command center, through the communications network established at that center, should contact each school frequently and regularly to report the status of the emergency. Administrators at those schools must remain in their buildings in order to provide the appropriate assistance.

Following the shooting at Oakland, communication with the

other twelve schools in the district was overlooked. Those schools did not know the gunman had been apprehended. They began locking doors and implementing emergency procedures in case the gunman tried to enter their schools. It was a full two hours later that the district contacted each principal to inform them of the situation.

Notification of other schools in the district may have impact on persons in those schools. If some students have brothers or sisters at the emergency site, those students should be given accurate information about the situation. In addition, teachers or other staff may have children or spouses at the emergency site. Those adults must be released to go to the emergency site. A procedure must be in place to provide substitutes for those persons.

If an off-campus emergency happens in another school district (as in the Pinecrest bus accident), staff in that district should be contacted for assistance until local staff can get to the scene. Although hospital and emergency medical staff are conscientious and caring in their efforts to help, school personnel will understand more about the types of information needed in the command center at the local school.

Closing School

Back at the school site, decisions must be made about the following days of school. If the emergency situation has had significant impact on the students or on the physical plant, it may be necessary to reschedule one or more school days.

The decision to close school, even for one day, should be made after considering all factors. Those factors can include such intangibles as community feelings and reactions and can include tangibles such as bullet holes in the chalkboards and bloodstains on the playground.

Following the Pinecrest bus accident, school was not closed. The distance between the accident and the school was a significant factor. Following the shooting at Oakland, the school was closed for two days. Fatalities, shock, and the need to repair were significant factors.

At Oakland, the first closed day was used to assist teachers and staff manage their feelings and fears while the maintenance crews repaired the cafeteria and classroom. The second day was used to assist teachers and staff prepare for the students' return. Both days were full working days for all school personnel as they prepared to help students understand their classmates' deaths.

At Winnetka, Illinois, school was not closed after a shooting. Factors in that decision included the isolation of the incident to one part of the building, concern for the safety of children who would be sent home, and the relatively small number of persons who witnessed the shooting. There was also concern that witnesses would be less reliable if they were sent home without debriefing.

The closing of school following an emergency will be a particularly local decision. Local school and district officials will understand the needs of the students, staff, families, and community. They can assess the need for repairs and need to prepare for the return of students.

Transportation

Transportation is a major part of the everyday operation of a school. Students come to school, move between campuses, and go home every day. Transportation becomes a special concern when students leave school for field trips or other special outings.

Transportation is a critical part of managing a school emergency.

There are several considerations in planning student transportation during a school emergency. Those considerations are related to the types of emergencies for which plans must be made. Even in school where the majority of students are "walkers," there must be plans for transporting all those students in certain situations (a chemical spill, for example).

Special transportation needs might be considered, as well. Following the Pinecrest bus accident, families of 47 students and adults had to travel a hundred miles to one of three hospitals. That mass movement of parents and spouses could have been coordinated with the State Patrol, local police, and sheriff's departments, thus making the travel much safer.

Conclusions

The major factor in decision-making during a school emergency is planning. District and school personnel will be better able to manage if they know the resources available to them, the responsibilities they and others have, and the basics of dealing with the safety of their students and staff.

School officials should also understand the stages in which an emergency evolves and the phases of management associated with the emergency. With that information, specific details can be managed. Although each emergency will be different, planning for the most likely events will minimize problems.

4
Using Technology To Meet Communications Needs During an Emergency

COMMUNICATION is a critical part of emergency management. Students and school staff must be told what to do. Parents of students and families of staff must be informed of the situation — and of the status of their family members. Law enforcement and emergency preparedness agencies must be notified in a timely manner. Community organizations that can provide services or that can help in the communication process must be involved. District board members must be informed, and updated information must reach them regularly. The press must be contacted and informed of the situation. Other individuals and groups will need information.

Information sharing during a school emergency will improve services to those who need them. It can mean the saving of life and property.

Using appropriate technological tools makes communication more effective and can also promote the public image of the school and the district. This chapter addresses common tools that can promote effective communication in the management process.

Telephones

The telephone is the most commonly used communications tool in schools. Most school telephone systems, however, are inadequate in two specific areas: (1) there are not enough separate lines to permit adequate communications during an emergency, and (2) telephone service is typically lost when electricity is lost.

Most schools have no more than two separate telephone lines into the building. In an emergency, two telephone lines will be inadequate. While the public is attempting to contact the school and those lines are busy, the school is unable to contact service agencies that may be able to help. In addition, the district is unable to contact the school to determine the extent of the emergency.

In an emergency, all telephone lines with published numbers will likely be in constant use. For that reason, all schools should have at least one private line with an unpublished number. That line can go directly to the principal's desk or to the desk of another administrator. That line can be used by district staff to contact the school and by school staff to contact the district or needed service agencies.

Many local telephone companies will work with schools during an emergency. Those companies are willing to drop additional telephone lines into a school if the emergency calls for additional communications capabilities. That process can better serve the schools if the telephone company is contacted as part of the school's pre-planning process. When the telephone company has been included in that pre-planning, its technicians will know what additional technology is needed.

When buildings are being built or renovated, the telephone company can put unused lines into a control panel somewhere in the building. Then, in an emergency, the telephone company can simply turn on those lines so that handsets can be attached.

When the telephone system relies on the power company, there can be serious problems for schools. If district staff knows that a tornado has been sighted and is moving toward one of the schools in the district, they must be able to contact that school. If the tornado has downed power lines leading to that school—and, as a result, the telephone system is not working—the district is not able to enhance the safety of its children and staff. For this reason, schools should request that their telephone service supplier investigate the possibilities for systems that are not dependent on the regular power system.

School telephone lines should use standard line jacks, such as the RJ-11 jack used in most homes. (The RJ-11 is the jack that unplugs simply by pressing a little plastic hook with a thumbnail.) If all telephone connections are standard RJ-11 types, handsets can be moved from one location to another in order to meet the needs of those involved in an emergency. In addition, many emergency medical service teams carry telephone handsets in their trucks. Those can be brought into the building and plugged directly into the telephone system if the school has standard telephone jacks.

In the emergency planning process, schools should inform emergency service agencies of the types of telephone jacks used in the building. Those jacks, both used and unused, should be marked clearly so emergency service personnel can find them. (The same should be done for all electrical outlets.) Discreet markers, such as colored circles, can be placed on the wall near the ceiling to indicate that a jack or outlet is located at the bottom of that wall. Emergency service personnel should be informed, during the pre-planning process, of that marking system.

Intercom Systems

Most schools have a public address system that permits communication from the office to the building or to individual classrooms. Many states have laws requiring that those types of systems exist and that they work properly.

Instructions for the use of the intercom system should be clearly posted near the intercom console in the office area. If school staff are not available, someone who is not a school staff member may need to communicate with or listen to parts of the building. This may be true in a hostage situation such as that in Montgomery, Alabama, in 1988.

Most school intercom systems are inadequate in one major regard: the teacher cannot initiate a call to the office. That means that a teacher who has seen an armed intruder in the hallway near his or her classroom must send a student out into that hallway to notify the office or must leave the students unattended to make the notification. Every school intercom system should include teacher-initiated communications with the office.

If the intercom system uses a handset rather than a wall-mounted speaker, communication with the classroom can be made without unduly alarming or frightening the students. The teacher can answer the call or can be told, through the wall-mounted speaker, to pick up the handset for special instructions. Those instructions can be delivered and a plan of action can be implemented without creating unnecessary fear or panic among the students.

In addition, students should be taught to use the intercom system. The teacher may be unable to initiate a call for help—a heart attack, a serious fall, or an armed intruder are among possible reasons. If students cannot call the office, they may find themselves in serious trouble also.

Bullhorns and Megaphones

Many schools have battery-powered bullhorns or megaphones. They are used at pep rallies and field days. They are also powerful tools for communicating with crowds during and immediately after an emergency. Greenwood School District found that there was no bullhorn at Pinecrest Elementary School the evening of the bus accident. The superintendent stood on top of a car and yelled, through cupped hands, as he tried to explain the situation to parents who had gathered in front of the school. At Oakland Elementary School, on the day of the shooting, a bullhorn was found in the office—but it had no batteries. It could not be used to call children, who had run into nearby woods, back to the campus after the gunman had been captured.

Many police officers carry bullhorns in their cars. School officials should involve those officers in the pre-planning process so they are aware that such communications tools are necessary in school emergencies.

It is also important to include a bullhorn (with charged batteries) in the kit taken by chaperons on field trips. In the event of an accident, it can be used to communicate with the students involved and with crowds that may gather at the site.

When purchasing a bullhorn, school staff should insist on re-chargeable nickle-cadmium (NiCad) batteries. In addition, the bullhorn should be hung on a wall in the outer office so that it can be found easily. It will serve little (or late) purpose if it is hidden in a cabinet and cannot be found.

Computer Communications

Personal computers have become common in almost every school in the country. Computers are being used in many instructional settings, and students are as at ease with these computers as adults are with television. Many schools have also begun the process of computerizing student data, such as demographic information, personal data, grades, and attendance.

Technology can be used in school emergencies. It must be emphasized that the use of computer technology for emergencies is simply an extension of its use for daily tasks.

The costs of computer hardware and software have declined markedly in recent years. Most schools can purchase a computer and software for use in managing student data. The system can be as complex as needed or as simple as possible. As the 1990s begin, more and more schools will automate student record keeping—and, thus, will improve the schools' ability to serve students and staff in emergency situations (as well as in daily operations).

Electronic Bulletin Board Systems

Telecommunications is becoming a major tool in the use of computers. Telecommunications requires a computer, a telephone modem, a telephone line, and a piece of software that asks for a telephone number to call. A computer should answer when the number is called. The process is simple and the cost is minimal.

A useful type of telecommunications in a school district is an electronic bulletin board system (BBS). In everyday operations, a BBS can be the means for sending memoranda to schools, receiving lunch counts from schools, and other sharing of information that cannot wait—or need not wait—for the courier. In emergency situations, a BBS can be the link among critical locations, emergency service agencies, and the schools.

A BBS is, physically, a computer with telephone modems. It waits for calls from other computers. When a computer calls into the BBS, it displays a screen from which the caller can select options for leaving or reading messages. The messages can be private (password protected) or public (posted to the public board). The concept is not different from the use of cork bulletin boards for posting messages to convention attendees.

For daily operation, schools will have pre-assigned times to call the BBS to collect and leave mail and messages. Messages can be left for persons at other schools, at the district office, or for other agencies that also have access (access is protected by a series of passwords) to the BBS.

For emergency situations, the school can use its computer to access the BBS and to continually update information for staff at the district office. In addition, other schools in the district can rotate calls to the BBS to determine the status of the emergency or to determine if action on their parts is required. Local emergency service agencies can also be given access to the bulletin board so they can monitor the ongoing events. If one of these agencies determines that it can provide a service, the user at that agency can press a key to "beep" the BBS at the district office. The district's monitor can then request more information and can pass it on to the school or other site.

The BBS can play an important part in providing services for students and parents when the emergency is off-campus. A school or district employee can take a portable computer to the emergency site or to the hospital, attach a telephone line to the modem in the portable computer, and then call the BBS from that site. Current information can then be posted to the BBS, and the school or district can share that information with those who are waiting.

Portable Computers

Districts should consider the purchase of one battery-powered (rechargeable) portable computer for everyday use as well as for emergency use. Portable computers can play an important role in services to students and adults involved in school emergencies — especially if the school maintains a computerized student database.

When an emergency occurs away from the school, a district staff member can take the portable computer to the emergency site. On the way to that site, he or she can stop at the school to pick up backup copies of the student database. That database can be loaded into the portable computer while the staff member is traveling to the emergency site. Once there, that database can provide valuable information about the students who may be injured. It can also provide information about the teachers and other school staff who may also be involved in the emergency.

Fax Machines

Even if the district does not own a facsimile (fax) machine, district and school staff should know what one can do and how to use it. A fax machine is nothing more than a telephone (with an RJ-11 jack and cord) that includes a copy machine. When one fax machine calls another, they can exchange copies of documents entered into the machine. One fax user can place a piece of paper containing the names, conditions, and room numbers for students identified in a particular hospital, and a copy of that list will be printed at the receiving fax machine — in just a few seconds.

Most hospitals have fax services (as do most hotels and motels). To take advantage of those available services, the local district must also have a fax machine. Portables are relatively inexpensive. If the fax machine is to be used for daily tasks, the district should consider a sturdy desktop version. (Almost all vendors of school supplies and equipment will permit the faxing of purchase orders. Many have toll-free fax numbers for that purpose.)

In off-campus emergencies, fax machines can provide an essential service. Hospitals can fax a copy of medical release forms for parents to complete and sign. The parents can, then, fax back the signed form. Medical treatment can begin immediately, without the hesitation associated with missing releases.

"Panic Buttons"

Some schools have "panic buttons" directly connected to the police or fire department. In most instances, the button is in the principal's office and school office staff are trained in its use. When pressed, it sends a signal to the police or fire department, setting off an alarm.

In some communities, the police respond immediately to the alarm and go directly to the school. In other communities, the alarm causes the police or fire department to call the school to confirm the emergency. In those cases, an unanswered call will result in action by the police or fire department. An answered call must contain a code word that indicates no response is necessary; without that code word, action is taken.

Beepers

Key people at the district level should have telephone beepers for emergency use — although many have them now for daily use. A beeper is a simple receiver with a unique telephone number (usually unlisted). When that number is dialed, the caller can give a brief message that is heard by the person wearing the beeper. The message usually includes a telephone number at which the call can be returned. Depending on the urgency of the message, the beeper's wearer will return the call.

Some districts use codes to indicate the urgency of returning the call.

Beepers are used, chiefly, to find people who are away from their work areas but who are needed for specific purposes. Without beepers, these persons may not know that they are needed until it is too late.

Cellular Telephones

Unlike a beeper, which is simply a receiver, a cellular telephone permits the user to communicate from any location in a community possessing cellular service — such as the front seat of a car. Cellular telephones can provide communications capabilities for district staff who are going to an emergency site.

Cooperating Agencies

Several agencies and local businesses can provide valuable assistance in managing a school crisis. The local emergency preparedness agencies have communications capabilities that go well beyond those of most school districts. These agencies can contact state and federal agencies when additional services are needed.

In many communities, private citizens with communications or transportation capabilities not available elsewhere are willing to assist in school emergencies. Likewise, local industry and business will provide assistance, if asked. When in the pre-planning process, ask these individuals and businesses if they will be willing to contribute and include them in the planning process.

Conclusions

As in all aspects of emergency management, planning for communications will result in better services to those who have been affected by the emergency. Pre-planning for support from the telephone company, the emergency preparedness center, the hospital, and other emergency service agencies will ensure the most appropriate response to an emergency. Planning for the use of computer technology will improve services and will improve the public's perception of the school's ability to provide for the safety of the district's students.

Communication is a crucial part of emergency management. Effective communication requires the right tools. Planning will ensure the appropriate use of those tools for each management task.

5
Dealing with the Media During an Emergency

THE ROLE of the print and electronic media during a school emergency is critical. Different media can provide different services to meet the school and district needs. This chapter describes the development of everyday rapport with the media, the management of information provided to the media during an emergency, and the continuing function of the media following an emergency. This chapter also describes the needs of the media in the school and the district. The development of a media plan, including policy statements and implementation of procedures, is also described.

The Reasons for Media Interest

"If they would only leave us alone and let us get out job done." This statement has probably been said by every person who has ever been approached by the media during the aftermath of an emergency. Although school personnel recognize the important role the media plays in the management of school emergencies, the pressures of dealing with media representatives in addition to dealing with the emergency can lead to increased stress levels.

That should not imply that the media's role is inherently negative. No school emergency can be managed properly without the help of the media, and the media cannot provide that help without the assistance of school and district personnel. That relationship is extremely important to both—and both must do whatever is necessary to ensure that the relationship remains positive during the stress of an emergency.

Following the Pinecrest bus accident and the Oakland shooting involving Greenwood students, the media made an immediate appearance. They asked school officials (what seemed like) endless questions and made (what seemed like) endless requests for information. No one was prepared to address all those questions or requests.

That experience is not unique. Questions are requests for information arise any time children are in danger. Stories about endangered children are news, and those who work with children must be prepared to work with the news media.

Even minor incidents involving children will bring local newspaper, radio, and television personnel. They will interview, record, and film in their efforts to satisfy the public's urgent need for information.

The larger the emergency, the more media are attracted — and the greater the problems in dealing with the media. The media are an essential part of the management process, however, and should not be regarded only in terms of their questioning. School and district staff who know how to deal with the media, how to use the specialized skills of the media, and how to maintain an effective relationship with the media will be able to manage the chaos which can follow an emergency.

Immediate Media Needs

Media representatives are often a very energetic group of people. The competitive nature of their business demands timeliness and accuracy in their reporting.

During a school emergency, however, the dissemination of information does not always maintain a high priority for school personnel who are trying to manage that emergency. This does not discourage media personnel from doing their jobs.

Questions are directed to anyone who exposes him or herself to a news reporter. School personnel may be unwilling to spend time delivering information to the media, and they may be unprepared to respond to many of the questions. Those who are in the midst of critical decision-making or who are victims of the emergency may view the media needs as interference in the management process, an invasion of privacy, or an attack on their right to find comfort among their peers and away from the eye of the public.

Yet both have needs for immediate communication with the public. The school has an obligation to provide information to the public, and the media is the vehicle for addressing that obligation — especially during an emergency. This obligation can be addressed with fewer problems if people are knowledgeable about the interaction of the media and a crisis emergency team. School and district staff must work with the media to ensure that the media become a proactive force in the management process.

Interaction with the Media

The first step in managing information dissemination is to assign one person to handle the media activities. The media contact person should report immediately to the emergency site or the command post established to deal with the crisis. He or she must begin collecting information and details to share with the media representatives. This person's primary task is the respond to media requests while other designated personnel complete the tasks associated with the management of the emergency. The media contact person should plan and organize interviews, press conferences, news releases, and contacts with local radio, newspaper, and television outlets.

The most critical information is that which will help eliminate anxiety and dispel rumors among the public. The dissemination of specific details concerning the emergency will help eliminate the chaos caused by parents and other relatives who immediately fear the worst for the children.

It is impossible to use internal resources alone to achieve this end. The media provide the best resources for reaching the most people. By determining the information to be disseminated to ensure fewer residual crises, the media contact person can become the key to the smooth flow of other management activities.

The contact person should be familiar with media procedures, should have access to all school and district personnel, and must have the ability to organize timely communication activities. He or she is the link by which the media can obtain timely and accurate information. Without such a contact, the media are forced to obtain that information by any means and from any school or district staff who make themselves available. That increases the chances that persons other than school and district representatives will be speculating about the events leading to and emanating from the emergency.

The first function of the media contact person is to collect as much information as possible — and as quickly as possible — without interrupting the activities of others who are handling other emergency tasks. Access to the command post is critical. A minimum of interruption can be achieved when the media contact person knows the details of the emergency plan and can go quickly to those persons in charge of each aspect of the emergency. From those persons, the media contact person can prepare facts to relay to the media.

The second critical task of the media contact person is to

establish an active and positive identity with media representatives. The contact person should establish a concrete relationship with the media. The media should know that he or she is the best source for accurate information, and they should not hesitate to approach him or her for that information. In return, the media contact person must recognize the needs of the media and should be prepared to help the media in meeting their various deadlines.

The First News Conference

The first news conference will provide the initial facts needed by the media to report their stories. The news agencies need immediate information to determine the scope of the emergency and to establish their plans to cover the story.

The news conference will be led by the district's media contact person. Other school and district personnel will not be available until this press conference is held, and it will be scheduled as soon as possible after the emergency has passed through its initial stages.

The first news conference will also enable the contact person to take requests for additional information needed by the media. It also provides an opportunity to announce a time and place for a formal press conference, where questions will be received by those persons engaged in managing other aspects of the emergency.

During that first meeting with the media, all information must be factual. Speculations, rumors, or possible future actions must be avoided. Also, this initial meeting should be used to indicate a place where the media can establish a base of operations. It can also be used to provide information about access to telephones, fax machines, restrooms, hospitality areas, and other local agencies involved in managing the emergency.

Care must be taken, during the first news conference, to avoid the release of unauthorized information. Schools may not be authorized to release the victims' names (those can be released by local hospitals or law enforcement agencies). Law enforcement officials, rather than staff members, can reveal information about any suspects involved in the emergency. School and district representatives must be careful to adhere to the laws and regulations stemming from the Freedom of Information Act.

The district should have guildlines by which it expects the media to seek information from school and district staff. Those guidelines should be disclosed to the media at the initial news conference. (Local media should receive copies of the guidelines as part of the planning process — and, in fact, the local media should be involved in the development of those guidelines.)

Media Guidelines

The district should share their guidelines with media representatives in an effort to ensure smooth media operations. Those guidelines may limit access to the campus, may limit the interviewing or filming of students without written authorization from parents, may limit interviews with school employees, and may establish other restrictions on the media.

At the same time, those guidelines can define the responsibilities of the media contact person; such as the timely delivery of accurate information, and can also explain how the media may request specific information or access to specific persons involved in the emergency management process.

Emergencies may create the need for temporary policies that deal with the specific emergency situation. Will employees directly involved in the emergency be able to meet with the media, considering the circumstances of the emergency? Will students be able to present a clear account of the situation without allowing their emotions to distort the facts? Will the interruption by the media of the instructional environment hinder recovery efforts? These and other unique considerations must be included in the formulation of guidelines for media interaction.

The Formal Press Conference

The media will be temporarily satisfied with the information presented in the initial news conference. A formal press conference, however, should be held as soon as possible after the emergency. The press conference should include all authorities involved in the management of the emergency and selected personnel directly involved in the crisis. This may include the district superintendent, the school principal, and a representative of the board of trustees.

The media contact person should know, in advance, to whom the media wishes to speak and should arrange for these persons to be at the press conference.

Depending upon the scope of the emergency, hospital officials, law enforcement officers, or emergency preparedness representatives may be included. No attempt should be made to answer any question beyond the authority of the members of the group. These questions should be directed to authorities in the areas being questioned.

An essential item at any press conference is a written press release. The prepared statement will eliminate many questions and will provide direction for the conference. If a written copy of all prepared statements is given to each reporter, it can assist the reporter with correct names, numbers, and details. Without the written statements, some of these details may be misreported. It will also present the facts from the perspective of the authorities involved in the management process.

Press conferences should be timely. Conducting a conference at 6:30 P.M. will not accommodate television reporters who may need information for the 6:00 news broadcast. The media contact person should also be available to do 6:00 A.M. radio spots and 11:00 P.M. television spots, or make arrangements for these to be done by other persons.

All interviews should be arranged through the media contact person. This allows for the combining of media requests and eliminates duplication of effort. A planned interview also provides for the selection of persons who are well informed and best able to communicate the appropriate information.

Specific Recommendations

In addition to the procedures related above, several other recommendations will help with effective media relations:

1. Always stay with the facts during a news conference.

2. Never use "No comment." If a question cannot be addressed, provide the reason it cannot be answered.

3. Never speak "off the record."

4. Be fair. All agencies must be notified of scheduled news conferences and all other newsworthy events. Also, do not permit exclusive interviews.

5. Give the message you need to give even if the right question is not asked.

The Media Plan

Developing a plan for dealing with the media is essential. During an emergency, critical decisions concerning media guidelines and responsibilities do not have a high priority. Yet the media will not wait for the school district to plan strategies and develop procedures to respond to them. Before any emergency happens, school districts should have an established policy statement, district guidelines, and communication networks in place to deal with the media.

Essential components of a district media plan include:

Policy statements. A media policy statement should contain at least two parts: an assurance statement and an insurance statement. The first assures the public that accurate and timely information will be provided in a spirit of openness and cooperation. This guides the development of the plan. The second statement should emphasize the protection of the main function of the school—student learning. This guides the plan by recognizing that all media activity is controlled by the intent to protect the learning environment as much as possible.

District guidelines. This section of the plan should include specific responsibilities of the media contact person and any guidelines which media representatives are expected to follow. These guidelines might include procedures for student interviews, regulations for access to the school campus, statements regarding staff interviews, and others.

One such guideline could be to identify district personnel responsible for position statements. Statements concerning the position of the school district on legal, moral, or ethical issues should be made only by persons responsible for policy-making.

Communication networks. Another important part of the media plan is the listing of media agencies, contact persons, and important telephone and fax numbers. In addition, the appropriate use of each resource should be identified.

Understanding the operation of the specific media representatives can benefit the school and district while providing timely information to those news agencies. Newspapers can provide more detailed and in-depth coverage than a thirty-second radio or television segment. Television can provide vivid action shots and frequent live reports. Radio coverage can enable a spokesperson to release information immediately that will help diffuse a volatile situation and can overcome the effects of unfounded rumors.

In addition to professional media resources and personnel, a listing of key communicators within the community is important. Feeding the "grapevine" with accurate facts can be as productive as using a professional agency in spreading information to the public. Often, such a word-of-mouth network can be very effective in countering false rumors.

Conclusion

Dealing with the media must be an organized activity. Do not get caught with your plans down! During an emergency, dealing with the media may seem like a low priority, yet all other activities are in jeopardy when no plan exists to provide the public with the information with which to begin the recovery process after a crisis situation.

The media can be a positive force in the district's efforts to manage a school emergency. In order to ensure that they are a positive force, the district must plan for their involvement—in both the emergency and in the planning for emergencies.

6
Dealing with Rumors During an Emergency

RUMORS emphasize the worst possible scenarios during an emergency. The potential for negative impact is so great that school and district staff may find that they spend more time managing rumors than they spend managing the actual emergency. The establishment of reliable communication networks can help dispel the impact of rumors. In addition, this chapter will discuss dealing with the sources of rumors and the involvement of the media in countering the negative effects of rumors.

The Source of Rumor

People are going to talk about an emergency. Information about a school emergency is shared at every opportunity. Without real facts to share, people may speculate, and those speculations soon become entwined with the facts and are not distinguishable from the facts. Although this is not done out of malice, rumors can cause many problems for those managing a school emergency.

Following the Pinecrest bus accident, rumors concerning the death of one child circulated in the community. The rumor caused much distress among the student's friends and relatives. At one point, the rumors were so convincing that school and district staff questioned the hospital staff about the accuracy of their information. Only a conversation with the child's parents convinced school officials that the rumor was unfounded and that the child was alive.

The sharing of information is one aspect of an emergency which cannot be controlled by rules or guidelines. The sharing of rumors, however, must be controlled in an emergency situation. Rumors may hinder the management process, may create a negative atmosphere in the community, and may lead the community to question the district's ability to manage the emergency. Even worse, rumors may lead the community to believe that the district cannot provide for the safety and well-being of their children.

Combating Rumors

When no information is available, people will share information. When accurate information is not available, rumors begin.

The best way to combat rumors is to provide with public with facts as soon as possible. One source of public information is the media. There are specific ways to involve the media in providing accurate and timely information to the public.

Rumors, however, must often circulate among persons closest to the emergency. Consequently, dealing with rumors involves internal, as well as external, communication.

Identifying all internal groups and providing for the dissemination of accurate information to these groups is essential. These groups include trustees, administrators, teachers, students, custodians, secretaries, lunchroom workers, and teaching assistants. When these people are accurately informed, the public is accurately informed. It is these people who are contacted in their neighborhoods, in their grocery stores, in their beauty parlors and barber shops, and on their telephones. They serve as primary sources of information.

Often, these people are ignored in the information chain. It is assumed that they already have access to accurate information or that people seeking information will go to the media instead of these people. Neither assumption is correct.

In managing rumors that originate within the ranks of school personnel, school officials should consider a very important rule: keep the staff quiet or keep them informed. It is obvious that the staff must be informed.

The clerical personnel who answer the telephones at the school and at the district offices must be kept informed. They must know which information can be shared and which information cannot be shared. They must also know which information is inaccurate so that they can address specific questions about it. The designation of a few persons to answer calls helps eliminate the passing of misinformation—which is often the source of rumors.

A faculty or staff briefing should be held before they are allowed to go home. The emergency could require that the briefing be held away from the school (and going to an alternate site can be a part of the emergency plan).

The use of key communicators within the community will also help deter rumors. A telephone chain or a debriefing meeting with a variety of community representatives will help spread accurate information. All members of the district's board of trustees and other persons directly associated with the school system should be included in that communications network. The public often relies on them for information about everyday operations. They will certainly be sought out during an emergency.

The media can also help control rumors. When a rumor is recognized, the media will cooperate to dispell it. The media can provide frequent updates to the public if they are given accurate information in a timely manner.

Public meetings are another means of controlling rumors. Providing people with the opportunity to ask specific questions and to receive specific answers will help in the battle against rumors.

Conclusions

The way to combat a rumor is to be aware of its presence. Officials must constantly listen for rumors and must find effective ways of eliminating them. Rumors can become as devastating as the emergency itself and must be dealt with accordingly.

7
Managing Parent Reactions

PARENTS will react to any situation that threatens the safety of their children. The initial reaction can include fear, anger, frustration, bitterness, blame, and guilt. The aftermath of an emergency may include lawsuits and other action by parents. Many parents will also react in supportive ways, and school plans should include procedures for incorporating that support into the management process. This chapter includes techniques for sharing information with parents, planning meetings in which feelings can be vented, and other activities that can promote positive resolution of parent reactions to emergencies that involve their children.

The First Reaction

It is very likely that a parent's first information about a school emergency will not come from someone at the school. When an emergency occurs, the news will spread through the community much more quickly than school or district personnel can contact individual parents. When the news is particularly dramatic, parent reaction will be equally dramatic.

Fear

Immediately upon hearing of an emergency situation, parents will fear the worst for their child. If they do not know what has happened or how their children are affected, parents will do whatever is possible to get to their child. The resulting chaos can be frustrating and dangerous.

When the local radio station reported that there had been a shooting at Oakland Elementary School, there were no other facts available. Parents who heard the news began to go directly to the campus. The distance between Oakland and the nearest major highway is about two miles, all of which is four lanes wide. Within minutes, the traffic along that street had come to a complete stop. Parents caught in the traffic jam abandoned their cars and ran to the campus. It was difficult for parents, district personnel, emergency personnel, and the police to get to the campus.

No one can fault the parents for their fear or for their attempts to get to their children. That is the first thought that enters the minds of all parents when their children are victims of a crisis.

When parents arrive at the scene of the emergency, there are only two things that can happen: they find their child safe and sound or they do not. The latter case presents a particularly difficult situation for school staff because they must confirm the parents' fears. If the child is safe, school staff do not have the luxury of sharing in the relief of those parents.

Anger

Anger follows the fear. The entire community—including parents—will feel anger at any situation that threatens the safety of children. That anger can be directed toward those who are responsible for the situation (if there is a clear responsibility identified). The anger can also be directed at society in general (especially when there is not a single person or group on whom direct responsibility can be placed). And the anger can be directed at school and district officials for allowing the situation to occur (because these officials have direct responsibility for everything that happens in the schools).

District and school officials should anticipate all forms of anger and should be ready to deal with it—and to let everyone else deal with it. They should not be afraid of the anger, even when it is directed at them. It must be recognized as part of the need to explain and understand tragedy, and it must be managed properly —for the good of the persons expressing the anger and for the good of the district and school.

There was, understandably, much anger following the shootings at Oakland Elementary School in Greenwood, South Carolina, and at Cleveland Elementary School in Stockton, California. The shootings were willful acts of violence that resulted in the deaths of two third-graders in Greenwood and five children between the ages of six and nine in Stockton. There was much less anger following the Pinecrest bus accident because it was an accident (although anger resulted following the release of the bus driver's poor driving record). Each school emergency will have its particular emotional character, and school officials should plan for dealing with it.

In Pinellas Park, Florida and Winnetka, Illinois, classes began the following day. Oakland Elementary School, however, was closed for two days following the shooting. During these two days, much happened. Two of the events directly involved parents. The first was a public meeting at which school officials listened and responded to the concern and anger expressed by parents and other concerned citizens. The second event was an open house after all the clean-up and maintenance tasks were completed. Parents and their children came to the school that afternoon to see that it was still the same school that had always been safe and secure for their children.

Both of these events were held because of the particular needs of the community, the families, and the students. Parents felt that school and district officials listened to — and heard — their concerns. Those officials were able to reassure parents that their children's safety was the prime factor in the educational process within the district. Parents and students were able to see for themselves that the school had been made safe again.

The anger directed toward the school and the district was dissipated, and the school was able to go back to its business of caring for the children who were sent there.

The Need for Details

Parents (and the rest of the community) will want to know the details of the emergency situation. Some information can be obtained from television, radio, and newspapers. It is extremely important, however, that school and district personnel provide first-hand details of the emergency and its management. That is a second purpose for holding a public meeting.

The public meeting should be arranged as soon after an emergency as possible. Emotions will be running high; the leaders of the meeting, though, must remain calm and must be understanding of the parents' emotions and needs. Parents must feel that they are being dealt with fairly and honestly.

School officials should recognize that the need for details stems from two basic emotions: parents want to know what has happened to their children and who is responsible, and parents want to know that their children will be safe again. Both areas must be addressed clearly and effectively.

The Need for Support

Parents must be given the opportunity to express their feelings if healing is to take place. In addition, parents need support in helping their children through the aftermath of the emergency. The school and the district can assist them in obtaining the services they and their children might need.

In Winnetka, Illinois, the principal contacted the five previous PTA presidents to receive their counsel and input on what the school should do in response to parent and student needs. Their suggestions were invaluable.

In Stockton, California, where many of the victims were of Asian descent, parents advised the school administration to have a Buddhist monk come onto the campus and sprinkle holy water in those locations were children had been killed. While this request may have seemed unusual to many people, it was essential in restoring parental confidence and support in the school.

Support from the district can include assistance in completing and filing insurance forms, obtaining continuing services for therapy or medication, and counseling parents in their efforts to adjust to and manage the changes that accompany particularly devastating emergencies. Support can also come in the school's willingness to provide special instructional programs for students dramatically affected by the emergency.

Conclusions

Emergency situations may occur through no fault of the school or its staff. The school may be considered as much a victim as those who are directly affected by the emergency situations. The school and the district office, however, cannot effectively argue that point when children have been hurt. Victim or not, the school and the district have the responsibility for planning the activities needed to help parents and students deal with the situation and its aftermath.

When parents and the community see that the situation has been handled in the best interests of the students, and when they have had time to analyze the situation, they can—and will—offer support to the school for handling a difficult situation in the best possible way. That positive support will be a direct result of the support provided by the school and the district.

8
Counseling and Other Continuing Services

TOTAL MANAGEMENT of a school emergency must include management of the events that continue beyond the emergency itself. Persons affected by the emergency will need debriefing, counseling, referral to service agencies, and other victim services. This chapter discusses many of the counseling needs associated with school emergencies. It also includes discussion of other continuing needs and services, and gives techniques and procedures for planning to meet those needs.

Immediate Counseling Concerns

The magnitude of a school emergency will affect the magnitude of needs of those who are directly involved in the emergency. School personnel should be aware that the way in which students, teachers, staff, and parents are affected by an emergency can vary a great deal, depending on the individual.

Each group may need debriefing and counseling services, and individuals within those groups may need additional services. The school and the district should be ready to assist as soon as the needs are identified.

Following the shooting at Oakland Elementary School, there was a critical need to help teachers deal with their feelings of helplessness, loss, and guilt. Those feelings showed themselves in varying degrees among the staff; all, however, had a need to manage those feelings. More than two years after the incident in Cokeville, Wyoming, one year after Stockton and in Winnetka, Illinois, counseling is still provided.

In addition to the need to deal with their own feelings, the teachers needed training to assist their students when they returned to class. Every teacher wanted help before being placed in the situation in which they would have to help returning students handle those same feelings.

Teachers are not the only school staff who might be in need of counseling and other support services. Custodial staff who work among students should not be asked to clean up the remnants of a disaster that has resulted in severe injury or death for some of those students.

When school resumes, everyone should be aware of the need to assist students in their talking through the emergency, its initial effects, and its aftermath. Whether teachers or counselors are involved in these activities, all must be particularly sensitive to students' needs and the likelihood that one or more may be traumatically affected by the emergency. Those who work with the returning students should know how to identify signs of extended stress and severe needs for continuing services.

If the emergency is particularly traumatic, there will be long periods in which counseling services will be needed—and there seems to be no defined pattern of predicting who may need much continuing services. More than a month after the shooting at Oakland, one teacher was particularly shaken when a student blew up his lunch bag and burst it with a loud pop. The teacher acted professionally in dealing with the student, but she was obviously disconcerted by the noise. There was an evident need for counseling, both for the teacher and the student.

Planning for Counseling Needs

When a school or district begins planning for emergency management, counseling is one of the key areas to consider. In preparing a school or district emergency plan, school personnel should contact professional counselors in the community or in nearby areas. These professionals should be involved in the development and implementation of the emergency plan. Most professional service providers will gladly work with the schools in emergency situations.

As part of the plan, professional counselors should know who to contact at the district level in case of an emergency. Likewise, school and district staff should know who to contact when such services are needed. When everyone is involved in the development of the plan, the needed services can be arranged with a minimum of delay and confusion.

School and district staff can find information about professional counseling by consulting with the department heads at local colleges or at the nearest state-supported college or university campus. Those departments often maintain a close working relationship with professional service providers in order to involve them in intern activities for degree candidates.

In addition to the services provided by professional counselors within the immediate area, schools and districts should take advantage of the church-related counseling services available in the community. Local religious leaders can provide group and individual counseling in addition to the personal counseling they offer their parishioners.

Additional counseling resources can be obtained from local departments of mental health. Counseling professionals in those offices are always willing to assist in emergency situations. They may be able to provide long-term follow-up activities as well as immediate assistance.

It is important to remember that, although school counselors are professional in the delivery of daily counseling services and effective in that role, they may have such strong personal bonds with those in the school that they may not wish to be involved in the counseling process. Then, again, they may wish to be very involved. The situation and the individuals must be considered by those on the decision-making team before determining who can and who cannot provide such services.

Whatever the immediate decision may be, school counselors will be the most important part of long-term counseling for many students and staff. Following a traumatic emergency, those counselors must be freed from many guidance and record-keeping tasks to they can work directly with those who need their counseling skills. Counseling staff from other schools may be needed on a full- or part-time basis at the school involved in the emergency. Those staff members should be assigned immediately.

Other community groups can be involved in the long-term counseling process. In Cokeville, Wyoming, counseling services are still being provided to victims more than four years after the event. Most of that involvement may not include actual counseling but may involve support and reinforcement activities. Some civic and community service groups may volunteer services for such support and reinforcement.

Community Support

Following a traumatic emergency in a school, students and teachers may be apprehensive about their counseling safety or about their ability to function within the school setting. Support can be planned in order to build confidence in the safety and security of the school. Let community leaders and business persons know how they can help, particularly parents. In Stockton, California, many parents patrolled the halls or screened visitors after the event.

Following the Oakland shooting, students, parents, teachers, and other staff had feelings, such as insecurity, fear, and anger, that could have interfered with their abilities to cope with the school setting. Businesses and service agencies provided an unanticipated source of support.

For example, restaurants and other food service agencies provided snacks in the morning and ice cream in the afternoon. They delivered these with a friendly and caring feeling, joking and playing with the students and staff. The police department, the sheriff's office, the state Highway Patrol, and other agencies visited the campus in shifts, walking the halls and providing a high profile for safety and security. They were also friendly and caring as they talked with students and staff.

The efforts of local business and the local law enforcement agencies contributed tremendously to the immediate healing needs of the students and staff within the school.

Other Continuing Needs

In addition to the need for counseling following a school emergency, there are needs for guidance services. These services may include assistance in completing and filing insurance forms for students and staff, assistance in filing for employee benefits by injured staff members, assistance in finding private counseling and care services, and assistance in finding other solutions to specific problems encountered by those affected by the emergency.

Children who are injured during an emergency may have school insurance or may be covered by a policy held by the parents. If school insurance is involved, the district staff members who specialize in the record-keeping for these services should be immediately available to assist the parents of these children. When the same insurance provider is involved, district staff may be able to assist in the collection of information needed to assure quick service to the persons involved.

One of the unanticipated side-effects of school emergencies can involve the reaction of some persons to apparent changes in achievement or behavior. As much as a year after the shooting at Oakland, discipline problems were dismissed by parents (who had been asked to come for a conference) as an adjustment problem resulting from the shooting. The students involved were in need of parental support but were receiving only excuses for their behaviors instead of receiving appropriate action. The students learned quickly that they could use their parents' overreaction to manipulate them and to cause difficulties at school.

If parents are made aware of the potential for such circumstances, both the parents and the school may have easier times dealing with behaviors that are and are not directly related to trauma caused by the emergency.

Conclusions

As with all aspects of managing a school emergency, planning for action before the action is needed will improve the potential for success in the management process.

Planning for counseling and guidance services must involve all who can help. Then, if an emergency occurs, the assistance can be delivered as planned, rather than arriving after school and district staff have had to go in search of it. The involvement of local civic groups, local businesses, and other local resources will further enhance the healing in the aftermath of the emergency.

9
Managing Public Relations Following an Emergency

THE PUBLIC RELATIONS FUNCTIONS of a school and district following an emergency can determine the support offered by the community. Public relations can include providing information and services to various persons and groups within the community, canceling specific events (such as staff evaluations) that might be adversely affected by the emergency, attending funerals, visiting hospitals, and other actions that will serve people involved in the emergency. This chapter describes the public relations needs and techniques that can help the school and district meet these needs — to everyone's satisfaction.

Form and Substance

The public relations functions of a school or a district usually involve a continuing communication with the public. Information about successful programs is shared through the local media, through newsletters, and through other communication networks. In addition, information may be shared in an effort to correct perceptions based on inaccurate information (unfounded rumors or information released in error). Public relations may also involve reshaping public opinion when that public opinion is based on facts damaging to the reputation of the school, the district, or the school and district administrators.

There are many opportunities, within the emergency management process, for inappropriate or ill-advised decision-making. School and district administrators may be making decisions based on false or incomplete information — information that may appear correct at the moment of the decisions but which is patently incorrect when the overall situation is reviewed. When such decisions are discovered to be inappropriate, the school officials must react appropriately. If they do not, public relations may be damaged severely.

Quite possibly, school and district officials will make all the appropriate decisions as they manage a school emergency. When that is the case, the public may or may not be made aware of it. If the school or district is unable to share the information relating to its appropriate decision-making, public relations may not be damaged, but those relations are not enhanced.

As cold and calculating as it may sound, schools and districts have two responsibilities in dealing with the public relations issues surrounding the management of a school emergency. First, school and district officials must do whatever is necessary to actively and appropriately manage the emergency. Second, these officials must "appear" to be doing whatever is necessary to actively and appropriately manage the emergency.

It must be noted that the second responsibility cannot be fulfilled if the first is not fulfilled. The public will quickly recognize when there is no substance behind a projected public image. It is possible, however, for the first to be fulfilled without fulfilling the second.

The purpose for suggesting that both these responsibilities must be met has nothing to do with promoting a false public image, whether for administrators or for the school or district as a whole. The purpose for promoting appearances involves community confidence and support for the local schools. But it must be remembered: appearance without foundation will be quickly and easily recognized by the public. Form without substance does not promote confidence or support.

Informal Public Relations

Disseminating information is a critical part of the public relations process. Part of that process must involve the media; the formal dissemination of information, however, is not the only component of public relations. The community will see and interpret the actions of school and district personnel as management of an emergency proceeds. Much information will be disseminated from the inferences drawn from these informal observations and interpretations.

Each school and district plan should include an awareness of the potential for informal information dissemination. The informal public relations process can enhance the public's awareness of the competence and completeness of the management process.

There are two major factors in managing positive public relations following an emergency. First, school and district personnel must manage the effects of mistakes made during the emergency.

Second, these personnel must manage the effects of successful activities completed during the emergency.

At times, taking a formal approach to addressing these factors will result in negative public relations. The public may feel that excuses are being made (when personnel are attempting to manage mistakes) or that the school, district, or individual staff members are attempting to "blow their own horns."

Managing Mistakes in Emergency Management

During a complex emergency situation, individuals will make mistakes in judgment and implementation. Typically, such mistakes will be minor and can be corrected with appropriate follow-up. Occasionally, a mistake may have significant impact on the success of the management efforts. In both cases, the mistake will be remembered by someone involved in the management process or in the community.

If someone who has responsibility for the management process —including the mistake—acknowledges the mistake and describes its correction, most of the negative impact can be dissipated without extended consequences. If the mistake is ignored or not corrected, school and district staff may spend an extravagant amount of time dealing with it later. The result is a public relations problem that will affect the credibility of the school and district in all other areas of operation.

One strategy in dealing with mistakes is to acknowledge the error and emphasize its correction. Attention should be focused on the correction and the positive impact of that correction. The correction must be appropriate and substantive. The emphasis must be appropriate and must focus on the substance of the correction.

The result is substantive action to solve a problem and the appearance of being in control of the situation although a mistake has been made. Parents and the community as a whole will feel better about the school or district capability to manage the safety of their children.

Managing Success in Emergency Management

In addition to managing mistakes within the overall management process, it is important to manage success within that process. As indicated above, it is important to do so in a manner that will enhance the school and district image, rather than promoting a self-serving image. The process for managing success must be appropriate for the event and the community.

One strategy for informal management of success is to keep the school and district staff informed of actions and reactions. These staff members will be—always—one of the best sources of factual information in the community. They can provide information in an informal setting and in a style that will not appear to be self-serving for the school or the district.

Managing the Remembering

Following an emergency, there may be factions within the community or within the school setting that want the situation forgotten as fast as possible. These persons may contend that continued counseling, acknowledgement of the anniversary, or other continuing activities will simply prolong the community's bad feelings about the situation and about the schools.

Such concern will typically come from a caring for the community and the schools; however, it may not come from an understanding of the healing process.

The community is always a reflection of its people, and people do not forget trauma easily. They need to reflect, to place the trauma in perspective, to remember, and to grieve. These are recognized parts of the physical and psychological healing processes through which people come to grips with the aftermath of serious crises.

The community must be given the opportunity to collectively reflect on the meaning of the events, to grieve for those who are lost, to rejoice in those who pull through, and to put into perspective the events that led to loss within the community. Part of the school and district effort must include participation in the community activities related to the emergency. School and district personnel must attend funerals, must visit hospitals and churches, and must participate in community efforts to relieve the burdens placed on families.

The school and district also have the responsibility to provide the opportunity for the community to come together in the aftermath of the emergency. The first anniversary of the event is an excellent opportunity to quietly and respectfully remember the events, those who were dramatically affected by those events, and those who acted to help. At that time, a final perspective can be focused and the community can be helped to understand the nature of the event and the healing that has come from it. The community can harbor feelings similar to those held by individuals. The anniversary is a time to remember that the community can let go of its anger, its fear, and its guilt.

The acknowledgement of the anniversary does not require a celebration. It can be a simple acknowledgement that the event has occurred and that people were affected by it. In Winnetka, Illinois, administrators began the new school year with a sunrise ceremony on the beach for students, parents, teachers, and staff. In Stockton, California, a Buddhist monk sprinkled holy water on the areas where children had been killed. These ceremonies, while perhaps unusual, were important to the healing process.

Little will be gained by continuing acknowledgements of the anniversary beyond the first year. There will be community members, however, who may call to offer support or to ask if there are ways in which they can help. The school must always be willing to listen and to guide these offers of support into constructive activities that can benefit the school and its students.

Conclusions

Informal public relations activities are an important part of managing a school emergency. When accurate information is provided about the management process, about mistakes and corrections within that process, and about the successes within that process, the community and individuals within the community will better understand the total attempt to manage the emergency for the benefit of all involved. In these circumstances, energy can be directed to actual solutions to problems within the emergency and its aftermath. Otherwise, much energy will be spent dealing with attacks relating to the lack of such information.

The most important thing to remember is, simply, that school and district staff must do the job *and* they must "appear" to be doing the job—in that order. The appearance must be based on real and substantive efforts to deal with the needs of those involved in the emergency.

10
Developing School Safety and Emergency Plans

AN IMPORTANT PART of managing a school emergency is the development of a school plan that addresses the major aspects of that management process. A school plan should include safety and emergency prevention procedures. Its development should be completed with the assistance of administrators, staff and faculty, parent organizations, emergency preparedness agencies, hospitals, emergency medical service agencies, the police, fire departments, industry, and other community groups. This chapter provides a step-by-step process for the development of school safety and emergency plans.

The Purpose of the School Plan

A devastating emergency may never arise in a particular school. Instead, minor crises may disrupt the day-to-day operation of the school. Although these minor events are not life-threatening, they can be handled better if an overall school emergency plan has been developed.

It may be difficult for parents and school personnel to believe that real emergencies can occur in their schools. It is important to overcome these beliefs and perceptions. The process of preparing school safety and emergency plans may seem like a meaningless exercise when it is first begun; however, the news of the past few years indicates that school emergencies are increasing—and are increasingly tragic.

Schools are vulnerable! They have been frequent targets of violence, and they have been victims of natural disasters (such as the deaths in New York State when strong winds blew down a cafeteria wall). Because school incidents involving death and injury do not occur in all schools, and they happen at unpredictable times, it is easy to take the attitude that such emergencies happen only at other schools.

No school is immune, and some are more vulnerable than others. For example, inner-city schools are more susceptible to events like gang shootings (such as those in Detroit, Los Angeles, Dallas, Cleveland, and other cities).

School plans should include prevention and preparation stages. For example, schools can establish visitor routines, position hall monitors, install and maintain communications equipment, and take other steps to prevent emergencies and to prepare for those that do occur.

In addition, schools should plan for the intervention and management of the emergency by the district. When district personnel arrive to manage the emergency itself, school personnel can deal with the issues involving students, staff, parents, and others who are directly involved at the school level.

Beginning the Planning Process

School plans should be developed by principals with the help of school personnel, parent groups, and community service agencies. The planning process should include all persons, groups, businesses, and agencies within the immediate community—it should include all who might be able to help and all who might be involved in causing an emergency that might involve the school. Advice from police and fire departments is necessary to insure coordination with these services.

The principal should invite appropriate persons to attend planning meetings and should share the planning activities with parent groups. More than one meeting might be needed, both for developing an adequate plan and to allow the involvement of everyone who can contribute. Meetings can be scheduled at different times of the day so that there will be the opportunity for more involvement.

As part of that planning process, members of the planning group should assess the specific needs of the school. Those should include the unique requirements of the campus and building, the flow of traffic to and from the campus, and other physical needs and resources. These should be available when the final stages of planning are begun.

Assessing the Needs and the Resources

How should a school protect its students and staff? How should a school prepare to manage an emergency when one does occur?

The first step begins with discussions among school staff. The purpose of such discussions will be to develop an awareness of potential problems. Staff members should list possible scenarios of disaster ranging from unwanted intrusions to natural environmental disasters. The end result should be the formulation of an action plan that addresses these potential problems.

School personnel should brainstorm without fear and without exaggerating potential dangers. The location of the school can be a contributing factor to the planning for specific dangers. Its proximity to industry or airports or communities with high crime rates should be considered. A list of potential dangers should be created. The items on this list can be ordered with regard to potential for harm and with regard to potential for occurring.

That list can, then, be shared with parents, community leaders and groups, industry, and others. These persons may be able to add to the list or may have recommendations about establishing priorities in dealing with the items on the list.

The second step in the planning process is an assessment of the school environment. A specifically appointed school safety committee can best address these issues. It should be comprised of representatives from the staff in the building as well as outside community members, such as police and fire representatives who have special training in emergencies.

The assessment should include the following:

1. The vulnerability of the school to certain hazards.
2. The adequacy of the school communication systems.
3. The training for staff, as prescribed in existing emergency plans.
4. The general conditions of the school, such as the location of exits and the visual access to parts of the building (as those relate to the building design).

In order to determine specific prevention and preparation procedures, the committee should review the following:

1. The building floor plan and campus layout.
2. School location in the community and its proximity to potential dangers.
3. Visitor and personnel traffic patterns.
4. Current visitor rules and procedures.
5. Personnel resources (employees and volunteers) with regard to potential dangers.
6. Intra-school and inter-district communications capabilities (including available technology).

7. The possibility of natural threats, i.e., hurricanes, tornadoes, earthquakes, etc.

After reviewing these items, a safety committee should have a feel for the relative safety of the school. The process is, in many ways, more important than the product. A heightened awareness of the relative vulnerability and security of the school will emerge from the group study. An indirect, but powerful, side-effect is that it helps such agencies as police or emergency preparedness groups focus on possible school problems. This will initiate the process of coordination of community and school safety planning.

Developing an Emergency Plan

Based on the assessment of needs and resources developed by the school safety committee or committees, an actual plan should be developed. That plan should be based on the list prepared in the assessment process.

The following items are commonly listed in such assessments:

Adequate investments in modern school intercom systems should be made so that emergencies are not compounded by a failure in internal communications. The principal should be able to communicate with any or all classrooms from most locations in the school. Teachers should be able, at least, to make instant contact with the school office.

Schools should pre-assign tasks and establish a clearly defined chain of command for personnel. Teachers, aides, parent volunteers, custodians, food service staff, and all others should know what they are to do and to whom they are to report in the event of an emergency. The plan should also include substitute teachers who may be working in the school at the time of an emergency.

A principal should always designate someone to act in his or her place before leaving the campus during the school day.

Staff roles can be developed by comparing needed tasks to the skills and capabilities of school personnel. Specific assignment of individuals to tasks will divide and organize the work. The list of tasks and individuals assigned to accomplish these tasks will be the basis for later staff training.

The school safety committee should not finalize the assignments until each staff member has reviewed his or her assigned role and accepted it. Staff members may feel that they cannot handle the assigned tasks, and they should have some input into the final plan.

During a school crisis, principals at other schools in the district should remain in their respective buildings during school hours.

The events may ultimately involve his or her school, and there is certain responsibility for students and staff at that school. Typically, if there is an emergency at one school, parents will begin picking up their children from other schools as well—especially if they have siblings in the school at which the emergency is occurring. The principal must be in the building whenever those parents need him.

The committee should look at internal and external communication and ask how well existing communication systems will work during an emergency. From a preventive point of view, intercoms are vital equipment. Their condition and capability must be assessed in terms of what demands may arise during an emergency.

In addition to assigning staff roles and upgrading or improving communication systems, the safety committee should prepare a list of items necessary for a school emergency list. During emergencies, common items are frequently hard to find. When those items are placed in an emergency kit, they are available immediately. A list of items for an emergency kit is included in Appendix A, which includes a sample school plan.

The school safety committee should also address the following:
1. A review of available safety equipment.
2. An off-campus gathering site for student who evacuate the campus during an emergency.
3. Modification of school traffic plans.
4. Designation of a media assembly site and school spokesperson.
5. A training plan for staff.
6. Deadlines for annual review and revision of the school plan.

The review of the safety equipment should include first aid kits, stretchers, bullhorns, and other items that might be needed during an emergency. An off-campus gathering site should be near the campus and should be known by all students and staff. This site may be critical if the school is unsafe and children are afraid. When designing modified traffic plans, it is important to plan evacuation traffic so that students can be routed to safety areas without interfering with incoming or outgoing vehicle traffic.

The media assembly site is important so that media representatives do not complicate the emergency management process. The media have specific needs and specific tasks that they must accomplish. It is in the interest of all that they receive timely and accurate information. Plans must include provisions for giving that information to the media.

A staff training plan which is rehearsed at certain times will ensure coordination and efficiency at the time of an emergency.

*Coordinating the School Plan with
District and Community Plans*

Emergency preparedness directors do not always take school plans into consideration when drawing up their own plans. Schools have very intense and very special responsibilities during an emergency. Community safety groups must know of these needs and the plans to meet them. Conversely, schools are frequently quite ignorant of the resources or plans already available in the community to help carry out these special responsibilities. For example, during both of the Greenwood emergencies, the school personnel failed to take full advantage of the communication and transportation resources available in the emergency preparedness headquarters.

A major part of a school safety plan must address coordination with the district plan. The school plan should be coordinated with local community plans also.

Finally, when the plan is completed, it should be disseminated to all parents, community leaders, and personnel who might have a need to know.

Additional Considerations

As principals and school staff begin to plan for managing school emergencies, there are several important points to consider. These are summarized below and may give some direction in the actual development of such plans.

1. Plans should be made for on-campus and off-campus emergencies.

2. At the beginning of each school year, a crisis management team should be established with members who will be the leaders in emergency situations.

3. Staff should know the location of (and mark clearly, if possible) all telephones and telephone jacks that can be used in an emergency.

4. The school should have a plan for informing the media of the emergency and for giving regular and frequent updates. A media area should be established in an easy-to-access location that is away from the main crisis control center in the school. The principal should designate one spokesperson to work with the district staff in preparing and sharing information with the press.

5. The school should establish a chain of command and a chain of communication so that important information is available to the

person-in-charge. Include, in these chains, links to the district office and district staff who will be on-site.

6. School staff should know and plan to use every possible means of communication. That includes all electronic and voice communications, crowd control devices such as bullhorns, community members, and the media. School and district staff should know who to contact and should take advantage of all communication channels.

7. All school administrators should expect rumors to be a problem. They must plan to counter rumors with accurate information disseminated through reliable channels.

8. The school should plan for support services. This may include food for those managing the crisis at the emergency site, counseling after the crisis for those who were involved, and other support services.

9. Teachers and other staff should be trained in basic emergency actions. This might include taking roll books or attendance cards with them if they must evacuate.

10. The school and district staff must plan for transportation of students away from the emergency site.

11. The school should prepare and maintain an emergency information kit.

12. Schools in the same district that are not directly involved in the emergency should plan to manage staff who have children involved at the emergency site. These schools should also plan to manage students who have friends or family at the emergency site.

13. Schools should devise a plan to assist in decisions to release students to relatives other than parents (in the time immediately following an emergency situation).

Conclusion

Everyone in the school has a responsibility for the safety of students and staff. The school's responsibility lies in planning for the prevention of emergencies as well as for the intervention and response strategies for the general safety of everyone in the school.

Planning should include the probable. Planning for all possible events is an impossibility; however, planning must be flexible enough to permit change when events are not anticipated beforehand.

11
Developing District Intervention and Emergency Management Plans

THE INVOLVEMENT of district staff is critical to the successful management of a school emergency. Advance planning for the roles of each district staff member is essential in that process. While the school's plan should be prevention-oriented, the district's plan must be intervention-oriented. District staff should take over the management of all significant components of a major school emergency, leaving the school staff to deal with the immediate needs of students and parents. This chapter provides a step-by-step process for the development of a district intervention and management plan.

The Purpose of the District Plan
   The district emergency is more a management plan than is the school plan. Each school can plan prevention measures and can collect, in advance, the resources for use in an emergency. At the time of such an emergency, however, the district should be prepared to take over the actual management of the emergency situation. The district plan should reflect that role.
   The role of the district office in an emergency situation cannot and should not be left entirely in the hands of school personnel. Sweeping decisions that can affect the whole community must be made, and officials in a particular school cannot make these decisions. Opportunities to take certain actions occur only once, and, if missed, these opportunities cannot be regained.
   Experience suggests a proactive involvement by the district office staff. This involvement must be planned and purposeful.
   The development of a district emergency plan can be organized into six major phases. These phases begin with the sharing of information to be used in the development of the plan and end with

the sharing of information to be used in the implementation of the plan.

Analysis of Resources

The first phase of planning involves the gathering of general and specific information which will be necessary for the building of a comprehensive, integrated plan. Many factors will have an impact on a school emergency at any given time, and it is important that district office staff analyze these carefully prior to formulating a district plan. A few of the factors involve political, social, economic, and geographical conditions within the district.

Each emergency will be different from others; however, there are problems common to most emergencies. These include, but are not limited to, the assignment of personnel and communications.

District office personnel must play a major role in handling a school emergency. In those emergencies in which the school was expected to carry out most of the major responsibilities in managing the crises, school personnel have felt abandoned by the district. That adds to the problems related to the long-term management of the emergency's aftermath.

District staff who have specific skills and knowledge should be assigned to manage specific part of the emergency process. A sample list of assigned roles for district staff is included in Appendix B, which includes a sample district plan.

In the pre-planning stages, district staff should review current policies and procedures regarding emergency management. The plan must have a foundation in these policies and procedures; otherwise, district staff will find themselves in untenable positions during and after the emergency.

District staff should evaluate the geographic resources available to each school in the district. At the same time, geographic liabilities should be assessed. For example, an industry near a school may be able to provide immediate medical assistance because it maintains a full-time medical program for its employees. These medical staff can arrive at the school more quickly than emergency medical services staff. That same industry, however, may manufacture toxic chemicals that could be the cause of a major school emergency.

Part of the geographic analysis of each school's needs and resources must involve transportation. There must be plans for the evacuation of students, for the arrival of staff from the district offices, and for access by emergency agencies. Alternative routes for each of these groups should be part of the district plan.

If a school is located in a hostile neighborhood where it is vandalized frequently, the residents of that neighborhood may have no "ownership" in the school. That lack of "ownership" could have negative effects during an emergency. Efforts should be made to incorporate community pride in the school so that community resources will be available in times of need.

The district staff must evaluate the communications capabilities of each school. Staff should work with each school and the appropriate agencies to provide adequate communications tools during a school emergency. District assistance may take the form of approaching the telephone company to provide extra telephone lines for each of the schools in times of emergency. The district may be able to guarantee payment of costs associated with such assistance by the telephone company.

District staff should understand and plan for the use of communication tools beyond the telephone support needed. Coordination of all forms of technology, including computers, instructional and public television, and others, should come from the district.

One of the most important parts of developing an effective district emergency management plan is coordinated with the individual school plans. The district plan should have components for each school, and each of those components must address the unique situations found in each school.

Development of the Emergency Plan

The district emergency plan should include assigned roles for district office personnel. When an emergency occurs and staff members have no specified responsibilities, management opportunities will be lost and unassigned personnel will be frustrated and feel useless. Personnel who are sent to hospitals, emergency preparedness centers, or to other remote sites should have been selected and assigned as part of the emergency plan. School personnel assignments to these locations enhance communication and facilitate problem-solving.

The superintendent should be at the center of the activity where decisions have to be made. He or she should be in a position to directly supervise immediate subordinates, meet with other officials, and provide for news conferences.

Some personnel act boldly under great pressure, while others are best suited doing tasks that require little risk or innovation. Making assigned roles from a list of tasks allows a district office to put capable leaders in the most crucial roles and giving supporting, but necessary, roles to other personnel. Individual skills, such as an ability to handle equipment, e.g. telephone switchboards or computers, are valuable. Counseling skills and writing skills can be utilized effectively if careful thought is given to the task list and the available personnel.

Assigned roles should include the responsibility for communication and for supervision of school personnel at the scene. If the emergency is in a school, one staff member should be in charge of the district office communication. All employees, administrators, secretaries, clerks, and other employees should come under the direction of that staff member. The switchboard, all phones, facsimile machines, and the networked computers should also be under the supervision of that staff member.

Each person assigned to a remote site, a command post, or the district office should know to whom they are to report. Employees should know and understand how their office equipment will be utilized during an emergency.

The use of district personnel in no way overshadows or reduces the importance of the school personnel role in the emergency. The two plans, the district and the school, should complement each other. School personnel and district personnel can easily share some responsibilities such as preparing for psychological or counseling services in the aftermath of the emergency. News conferences frequently may be shared by school and district personnel. That is the reason why close coordination of the two plans is necessary.

In addition to personnel resources, communication becomes critical during an emergency. It is important to have alternate communication systems available for the transmission of vital information. Telephones alone are inadequate, especially in schools or at sites where limited lines are available. Cellular telephones, portable facsimile (fax) machines, and compters with modems should be available for emergency situations. An emergency plan must also provide alternatives for crises, such as natural disasters, in which all telephones and other electronic communication are disabled.

While the staff is developing its plans, it should brainstorm about possible scenarios of emergency conditions and how they could be best handled and what resources need to be available. To make this job easier, emergencies can be divided into categories such as on-campus and off-campus. Then, within these categories, different types of situations can be imagined, such as those in which the school must be evacuated or the children kept within the school.

Most school districts have some sort of emergency policies or regulations or procedures for managing emergencies such as tornadoes or bomb threats. These plans should be reviewed carefully for possible revision if they require school board approval to change them. This review should include the school emergency plans also.

Coordination of the District Plan with School and Community Plans

The time to secure resources is before those resources are needed. If no plans are made for resources prior to an actual emergency, management opportunities will be lost — and that could result in tragic consequences.

As the school and the district office develop their plans, it is quite helpful to hold joint meetings of the school representatives and the district office staff to be sure that either the school or the district office does not presume to take on the responsibilities of the other. In the process of development of the district plan, meetings with community leaders, fire department officials, police officials, and local government officials can make the plan more effective.

If the police, fire, and emergency preparedness people know what the district will do in the emergency, their own plans can be adopted to avoid a duplication of effort. Meetings will help community agencies to be prepared to assist the school district in managing an emergency.

In Greenwood, opportunities were lost because the district had not planned for the involvement of the police and other service agencies. In the Pinecrest bus emergency, the superintendent spent several hours trying to give information as he shouted to a large crowd of parents, media, and citizens without the aid of a bullhorn. The police cars at the school were equipped with built-in bullhorns and could have minimized the communications problems if they had been used to address the crowd. Coordination is indeed important, not only during, but also before, the emergency.

Making the Plan Public

As with school emergency plans, the district plan must be developed with the involvement of as many persons and groups as possible. The plan will be more comprehensive and effective when many different views are considered in the planning phases. These views can be consolidated by a relatively small group of district staff who have the responsibility for developing the final plan.

After the plan is developed, the district should inform all schools and community groups of the plan. The plan should be published and disseminated to all persons and organizations that might be able to contribute to the management of an emergency. It should also be distributed to all persons and organizations that might contribute to the creation of a school emergency.

A summary version can be shared with the local media, for publication or public discussion.

Training All Staff and Volunteer Personnel

One of the critical components of a district emergency management plan is the training of staff, both district and school. That training should cover all the components and relationships of the school and district plans. The plan cannot be implemented properly unless school and district staff know what is in it and what it means.

All district staff, including temporary and volunteer personnel, should be trained in the implementation of the plan. Each should know what is expected and to whom to report in the case of a school emergency.

The plan should be put in a ready-reference format for district office use and for school employees. The ready-reference handbook can be the basis for district inservice and training.

This training can include a mock disaster drill coordinated with local emergency preparedness groups.

Sharing the Plan with State and Local Agencies

State agencies, such as the state department of education, should also have a copy of the plan. In fact, many states now require districts and schools to prepare emergency plans and to submit these to the department of education for review.

The district plan should be shared with the state law enforcement agencies, such as the highway patrol. Many of these agencies can contribute great resources in the management of a school emergency, and many are willing to do so as part of the comprehensive plan. If those agencies have a copy of the plan—and, better yet, if those agencies have been involved in the development of the plan—they can begin providing services immediately, without waiting for a call for assistance and without the time required for an assessment of need.

The District Role in Managing a School Emergency

School emergencies evolve in three basic stages. The first is the initial crisis stage that includes the event and the immediate results of the event. The second stage includes successive events related to the original event; some of the successive events may also be classified as crises. The third is the follow-up stage in which the district must deal with the aftermath of the original event. The follow-up stage can last for a long period of time as support and continuing care are provided the victims of the emergency.

The initial crisis stage starts when the emergency occurs and district staff are notified. In that stage, district officials inform other district staff of the emergency and those staff members report to their assigned stations. District officials establish a command center and begin gathering facts. The following information is the minimum required to begin the management process:

1. The extent of the emergency.
2. The names of all who are involved in the emergency.
3. The location and condition of those injured in the emergency.
4. Other information necessary to effect appropriate management of the event.

The district staff in charge must then establish a communications network that includes the efficient use of telephones, facsimile machines, computers, and other available technology. That communications network should also include contact with the appropriate personnel, local service agencies, and groups within the community that can assist in the dissemination of accurate information about the emergency and its aftermath.

District officials then begin the process of making decisions about the immediate needs resulting from the emergency situation. These needs may include the following:

1. The re-assignment of staff based on the nature and extent of the emergency.
2. The closing of one or more schools and the length of those closings.
3. The transportation of students, staff, parents, and others who are to be evacuated.
4. The scheduling of news conferences and the identification of information to be disseminated through those news conferences.
5. The assessment of need for support services, such as food, shelter, access to the command center, security and safety of staff, counseling, and others.

6. The communication of decisions through the appropriate channels.

The successive events phase includes the on-going management activities that must take place after the determination of immediate needs has been made. It follows activities that have provided for the safety and care of all who were involved in the original event.

Management of successive events will include, but will not be limited to, the following:

1. District officials communicate with the families of those directly involved in the emergency.
2. District officials plan news conferences and media interviews to share specific information about the causes and potential effects of the crisis.
3. District officials begin planning for a return to the normal routine; steps are taken to re-start school; these steps must include plans for returning the physical plant to its original state.
4. District officials assure parents and the general public about the safety of the children in the school.
5. District officials lead the effort to counter the negative impact of unfounded rumors.
6. District officials manage continuing events resulting from the emergency.

The aftermath of a school emergency is not limited to a few days following the actual event. Some of those involved may need extensive medical assistance or extended periods of grief. Some may need continuing counseling services as a direct result of the emergency.

Emergencies do not end as quickly as they begin. The district has a long-term responsibility to assist those who are affected by a school emergency. That long-term responsibility may include the following:

1. The assignment of a full-time counselor to the school.
2. Assistance in securing private counseling service.
3. Assistance in securing physical therapy services.
4. The provision of special modifications to the school to accommodate physical needs that result from the emergency.
5. Assistance with completion and filing of insurance forms and forms for extended services needed as a result of the emergency.
6. Other services and activities to deal with the continuing needs of students, staff, and families affected by the original event.

Conclusions

The district's role in a school emergency is one of intervention and management. As district staff take over the management of an emergency, school staff can turn their attention to the specific needs of students, staff, and others who are involved directly in the emergency.

The district's role supports the school and the community. The active involvement of district personnel in appropriate action assures everyone that students' safety is the primary consideration in the management of schools. Without that active involvement, the district will not maintain the public's trust in the care of their children.

12
Developing Staff Training and Inservice Activities

AN ESSENTIAL ELEMENT in the successful management of a school emergency is the response of school and district staff in the initial emergency stage, in the management stage, and in the follow-up stage. Staff training, including administrators, faculty, staff, custodians, food service employees, and others, is essential in planning for emergency management. Training should include prevention as well as intervention techniques. Specific situations, such as safety during teachers' visits to students' homes, are included.

Training and inservice activities should be planned to meet three distinct needs: (1) faculty and staff must know how to prevent certain types of emergencies; (2) faculty and staff must know how to respond when an emergency occurs; and (3) faculty and staff must know how to deal with the aftermath of an emergency. The first two needs require training before an emergency occurs, and the third requires inservice after an emergency has occurred.

Training Before an Emergency

The training of staff to deal with school emergencies should involve everyone in the school. There should be activities for teachers, aides, librarians, counselors, custodians, food service staff, secretaries, clerks, substitutes, and volunteers. Different training activities may be planned for various combinations of staff members; however, every staff member should have a basic idea of the responsibilities of others. There should be at least one training activity that includes everyone.

The activities should include training for the prevention of emergencies and for action during an emergency. During all inservice and training activities, emphasis should be placed on the safety and well-being of the students.

The first major consideration in staff training for the management of school emergencies is an awareness of the school and district emergency plans. Inservice activities should include discussion of those documents and their impact on staff in dealing with potential emergencies.

The school and district emergency plans will usually contain specific emergencies for which specific actions are pre-planned. These may include fires, tornadoes, bus accidents, intruders, and others. Each of these topics should be reviewed in detail, with activities that will reinforce an understanding of actions to be taken.

Tasks and roles assigned to staff should be discussed in detail. Every staff member should know what to do when an anticipated emergency arises. In addition, each staff member should know what do to when an unanticipated event occurs. The training should reflect the flexibility built into the school plan.

Teachers should know to train their students to evacuate the building and playground. Teachers and students should know of planned re-grouping areas away from the campus; in an emergency that requires the rapid evacuation of the campus, everyone should know to re-group at these alternate sites. In addition, teachers should be instructed/trained to take their class rosters or roll books whenever an evacuation is required. These will assist in accounting for students when re-grouping has taken place.

Teachers should know what to do when they see activity that is different from that which might normally be expected. There should be specific procedures for reporting such exceptions to the office—and for reporting these as soon as possible.

In times of emergency, not all people respond with calmness and appropriate behaviors. School staff should know what to expect if one of their colleagues—or themselves—over-reacts or panics in an emergency situation. The principal or other person in charge must act to remove that person from the scene before the panic spreads.

Inservice activities may also include self-defense training for school staff. Such training, however, must include common-sense training so that school staff do not risk their lives because they believe they can subdue an armed intruder—or something like that. The self-defense training may, in fact, do more for self-concept and self-discipline than for interventin in a dangerous situation.

Training should address the responsibilities that each staff member has in terms of dealing with an emergency. It should also address the liabilities incurred by taking certain actions. Staff should know what they can reasonably be expected to do and what they can reasonably be expected not to do.

Staff members should know the limitations imposed on them by the Freedom of Information Act. They must know which types of information are confidential so that they do not inadvertently disclose them.

On the other side of the confidentiality issue is the teachers' need to know specific facts about students that might help them manage an emergency involving those students. For example, some parents do not notify the school that their child is epileptic and prone to violent seizures. If the child were to have a seizure in class, and the teacher were unaware that the child had epilepsy, the teacher might not be able to deliver the special services needed to prevent injury or death. In those cases in which special circumstances are known, individual teachers should be informed.

Training should include basic first aid and CPR (cardiopulmonary resuscitation). Every school employee should have some skill in assisting injured persons while waiting for emergency medical personnel. Other training may also include techniques for dealing with students involved in acts of violence, drug-related behaviors, suicide, and other events that may become specific emergencies. School administrators or district administrators may determine other topics for inclusion in pre-service and inservice activities.

Staff training should take place immediately before school begins for the new school year. A refresher session should be presented near the beginning of the second semester.

Inservice After an Emergency

Following a major school emergency, it is necessary to brief all staff about the emergency and its effects on the school and community. That session can also provide counseling services to the staff members (if the emergency has been particularly traumatic).

After-the-fact inservice activities may include training for counseling students who will return to school after the emergency. It can also include techniques for assisting parents who have questions and fears about the safety of their child. Teachers should also know when and how to make referrals for changes in behavior related to the emergency situations.

The inservice activities should include plans for returning the school to normal operation. These plans will include re-opening schedules, make-up days, and special considerations for those who were directly affected by the emergency. It should also include a post-assessment process, asking the questions: What seemed to work? What didn't? What could we do differently next time? What lessons did we learn?

Activities for Parents

Near the beginning of each school year, school staff should share, with parents, information about the potential for school emergencies. The most common emergency — at least, from the parents' point of view — is the closing of school because of weather. Parents should be notified, early in the school year, of procedures to be followed by the school for cancelling school, for early dismissal, and for delayed starts.

Parents should also be aware of off-campus re-grouping areas in the event of an evacuation. They will, then, know where to go to find their child in such an emergency.

One of the most important items to include in parent activities is the procedure for early dismissal of a student. Parents should understand the process and its importance to the safety of their child. Parents should provide the names of persons who have permission to pick up their child in the event of an emergency. The school, then, has an obligation to keep the child until someone on that list shows up.

Conclusion

Staff training, student training, and parent training for the management of school emergencies should focus on balance — keeping things in perspective so that events can be balanced against the safety of student and staff. Activities should reflect that balance — and must provide for the safety of all.

13
School Safety as a Function of School Design

SCHOOL SAFETY can be enhanced by building schools with safety in mind. Architectural and environmental design of schools, campuses, and ancillary structures have a dramatic effect on student and staff safety. Efficient supervision requires visual access to all areas of the buildings and grounds. The discussion includes line-of-sight supervision from the central administrative area, communication needs within school buildings, traffic flow and control, site selection, and other factors that can affect the overall safety of those who attend and work at the school.

Site Selection
The location of new schools should be viewed with maximum safety and security as a key factor. Consideration should be given to large-scale potential for disaster and to small-scale potential for emergencies.

In looking at the large-scale possibilities, communities should look at natural environmental factors as well as man-made factors. The potential for natural disasters such as earthquakes near fault lines, flooding near rivers and dams, storms near coastal areas and in the Midwest, and other environmental factors should be considered in site selection for every school.

School campuses should be placed in areas that are not likely to become industrial parks or major thoroughfares. With proper community planning and zoning, schools can be located in areas that will provide an environment free of potential for man-made disasters such as chemical spills, airplane crashes, and others.

Site selection should also be based on factors such as potential for crime and drugs. Other factors relating to neighborhood crime should be considered.

School Buildings

In the past, the concept of school safety and security was to lock the doors and the windows. Today, safety and security concepts include terrorism, kidnapping, armed intruders, student violence, and other intentional disruptions of the school setting. Safety and security also include management of the facilities to decrease the opportunities for individual violence and intimidation and to reduce access to drugs and other items that may result in unpredictable changes in student behaviors.

In existing schools, safety and security have been promoted through the use of monitors, guards, locks, lighting, and security patrols. Metal detectors and other devices have been used in attempts to reduce the numbers of weapons on campuses. Some campuses even have live-in security guards. Dogs have been used in attempts to reduce the amount of drugs on campuses. Some schools use armed guards to enhance the safety and security of their campuses.

When a district is contemplating a new school, school design should be an important factor in planning a safe and secure environment. Visual access by school supervisors is important in maintaining that environment. Schools should be designed so that administrators or monitors have maximum visual access and can see down several hallways from one point. Such visual access can be provided if a school is built with the administrative offices in the center with halls radiating from that center. The halls should be free of furniture (except low benches, perhaps) and should not have alcoves into which students or intruders can step to get out of the line of sight. Lockers, if they are to be placed in the halls, should be flsh with the walls.

Classrooms should be designed so that the teacher has visual access to all areas of the room. Cabinets and closets should be flush with the walls and should not create areas that are not directly observable from any other point in the room. Classroom doors should have windows that are left uncovered. Visual access into a classroom is important in managing an emergency situation that may be occurring in the classroom. Windows to the outside should be wide enough to permit evacuation of the classroom, if necessary. Those windows should open easily and should be designed to permit exit by handicapped students as well as adults.

Each classroom should be part of a school-wide communication system that permits classroom-initiated calls to the office. Intercom systems should provide access to each classroom from remote communications devices that can be carried by the school administrator as he or she moves about the building.

Public access to the building should be limited to the entrances at the front of the building and should require each visitor to stop at a reception area. Someone should be at that reception area at all times during the school day. That entrance could, in fact, lead directly into the administrative office area.

All doors leading to the campus must be secure but must be unlocked at any time there are students or staff out of the building. Although a major concern about school safety involves keeping intruders out, that concern must also involve letting students back into the building if there is an emergency on the school grounds.

Restrooms can be centralized near the hub of a school built with halls radiating from a central hub. Restrooms should be similar to those found in shopping malls; that is, access is through an open entrance with privacy assured by the placement of walls to obstruct vision from outside. The open entrances and a relatively open interior area will permit auditory monitoring from the hall areas as well as quick access for visual monitoring. Such a design can reduce the abuse of restroom areas for illicit activities.

Security lighting can be placed at strategic points in the office areas, hallways, and classrooms. The use of security lighting has been questioned by some schools; in certain school districts, campuses are lit to deter crime. Another school of thought espoused by the San Diego Unified School District suggests that all the lights be turned off to deter crime. Then, when you see the light turned on in some portion of the campus, you know you have a potential problem.

Campus and Grounds

The school building should be placed on the campus so that it controls access to the outdoor student areas. Access to the campus and playgrounds should be controlled by fencing or other security devices.

A school campus should be free of shrubbery and trees that permit persons (students and intruders) to hide on or near the campus. Shrubbery and trees can be placed on the campus to add the necessary shelter from the sun and to enhance the appearance of the campus without contributing to safety and security problems. Shrubs and trees can be placed individually (rather than in clusters) and can be placed in otherwise open areas (rather than along the perimeters of the campus).

Fences can be placed around the campus to add security. Shrubbery should not be placed on either side of these fences because of the potential for intruders to hide just outside these fences. Whenever possible, the grounds on both sides of school fences should be cleared for several yards so that possible intruders can be seen as they approach the fence. Such clearing reduces the opportunity for intruders to enter the campus without being seen.

The proper placement of lighting fixtures on the campus can reduce the potential for vandalism and break-ins. Security lights should be placed so that all areas of the campus are visible by passers-by as well as by security patrols.

Several schools have experimented with the elimination of security lighting, both inside and outside the building. The administrators for these schools have contended that such a practice places the entire campus and building in total darkness at night, making it difficult for vandals and thieves to see where they are going and what they are doing. It also requires such intruders to provide their own lights if they are serious about their work, and such lights are easily seen by passers-by and security patrols. In addition, the elimination of security lighting reduces costs.

Ancillary Structures

Ancillary structures can include gyms, warehouses, athletic facilities and fields, and others. These should be placed on the campus so they provide the least obstruction of vision around the campus and the least obstruction of vision to the areas adjoining the campus. Some obstruction will always exist. Plans should minimize that obstruction.

Traffic Control

Parents and politicians are the first to complain when their access to a campus is impeded by security measures. They are also the first to demand more security after an emergency has resulted from an intrusion on the campus.

Access to a school campus by the public is important. Traffic control is important during the times immediately before and after the regular school day. That traffic can be naturally controlled by the creation of driveways and access roads that direct traffic to the appropriate stopping and pick-up points.

Access to the campus during the regular school day is an important factor in school security. Persons who enter a campus in order to create or participate in the creation of an emergency will always want to leave campus at some later time. If all access leads to or past some point where entry is noted, intruders are less likely to enter and are less likely to enter without detection.

Conclusions

Schools can provide natural deterrents to intentional intrusions and can provide protection from natural disasters and accidents if they are planned carefully. Location, line of sight, access, and traffic control are a few of the issues to be considered in this planning. All aspects of a building program should include evaluation and assessment based on safety, security, and common sense in managing the school and the outside world's contact with that school.

APPENDIX A

A Sample School Emergency/Safety Plan

THIS APPENDIX includes a sample school emergency/safety plan. It has been compiled from plans submitted by various schools, using the best components of each of the individual plans. The sample plan includes special considerations related to location, proximity to potential hazards, and special facility needs.

A school plan should be comprehensive yet not overly complex. If a plan is too detailed, it will not afford the flexibility needed for unanticipated emergency events. If it is too complicated, staff and students may not be able to remember what to do in specific cases. It is best to plan well, with the help of those who can contribute, and to implement with care so that everyone feels safe and everyone knows what to do to maintain that safety.

Sample School Emergency/Safety Plan

A fictitious school, Kidville School, has developed an emergency/safety plan that addresses its specific needs. Each of the following sections includes information gathered in a needs assessment and action taken to meet these needs. The process involved administrators from the school and the district, teachers and other school staff, parents, police officers, emergency medical services staff, hospital staff, the local emergency preparedness officer, and other persons who could provide assistance in emergency situations. The process for developing this plan is described in Chapter 10.

The school's role is one of prevention and safety. The plan provides measures for the prevention of emergencies that can be anticipated and for the general safety of students and staff. It anticipates the district's role of intervention and management should an emergency occur.

The Building and Campus

Kidville School is an elementary school, housing approximately 540 students in Grades K–6, with approximately 40 four-year-old preschoolers. It is in a residential area and faces a busy street that provides access to all the residential streets in the neighborhood. The main hall of the building parallels the street, with three additional halls perpendicular to the main hall.

The playground area is directly behind the building and is bordered by a street. The playground area is fenced along the street but is not fenced along the property boundaries on either side of the playground.

The school office area is in the front of the building, on the main hall. The only telephones in the building are in the office and in the food service area, which has a line separate from the main telephone lines. The telephone system has two published numbers that rotate through four handsets. If the power goes out, the telephone system does not function.

The school uses a personal computer for keeping student records, including attendance and grading. In addition to the computerized student records, the school keeps a paper record for each student. The paper record contains a photograph and immunization records. Additional information is also kept in the paper folder, but most of it deals with academic assessment and instruction.

Classrooms have only one door, each of which has six glass panes. The windows in the classroom are above the heating units. Only the buttom section of each window opens, pulling inward. The resulting opening is eighteen inches high and thirty-eight inches long; however, the open section of window reduces the actual height of the opening to just twelve inches. Access to that opening requires going over the open section of glass.

Each classroom has one speaker attached to the public address system in the school. All speakers work. There is no teacher-initiated call system.

Access to the building is through eight different locations. The front of the building has one entrance that comes into the lobby area at the office. Each end of the main hall has a set of double doors, and each hallway has a similar set of doors that open to the playground area. Another set of doors gives access to the food service area (the middle of the east wing), and another set gives access to the maintenance area, which also houses the heating and cooling systems (the middle of the west wing).

The school does not use on-site security guards.

Neighborhood Hazards and Havens

Private houses are the only buildings within a two-block radius of the campus. Several apartment buildings are within walking distance to the campus. Six churches are within four or five blocks of the school.

The police department is two-and-a-half miles away; a fire station is only one mile away; the local hospital is six miles away, on the other side of town. A rescue-squad unit is located at the local fire station.

Within a mile, to the east of the campus, is a major traffic artery on which there are several shopping centers and small businesses. Within a mile or so, west and north of the campus, are several large industries that manufacture textile products, automotive parts, and agricultural pesticides. About two miles southwest of the campus is the local airport, which is not large but does have regular service from regional airlines. There are no major railroad beds near the school, but all the large industries have rail access from a major line that is about seven miles to the north of the campus.

Traffic and Transportation

Visitor traffic and parking is limited to the front of the building. Because the front entrance is the only visible entrance from the front parking area, most visitors will use the front doors without question.

Teacher and staff parking is in a separate area at the west end of the main hall. Teacher and staff access to the building is through the doors at the west end of the main hall.

School buses deliver students to the east end of the main hall. The buses use a circular drive that is separate from public access to the main parking area.

Because the street on which the school is built is reasonably busy during the working day, district office staff know several alternate routes to the school. These routes use less-traveled streets and provide quicker access to the campus from the district office.

Responding to emergency calls, police can arrive at the school in under seven minutes, the fire department and rescue squad can arrive in under four minutes, and ambulances from the hospital can arrive in under fourteen minutes. In an activity coordinated with the local emergency preparedness agency, a helicopter was landed in the playground area without difficulty (although power lines and telephone lines were moved underground after that exercise).

Safety

Barricades are placed in the access drive to the teachers' parking lot and in the driveway to the bus circle after school has started each day. The only unblocked traffic entrance to the campus comes directly to the parking area in front of the building.

The doors at both ends of the main hall are locked, after school starts each day, so they cannot be opened from the outside. Panic bars permit these doors to be opened from the inside. The outside door to the maintenance area is locked at all times and can be unlocked only with a key. All other doors are unlocked during the school day because there are students on the playground during most of the day. Evacuation of the playground (because of an intruder or other danger) necessitates access to the building without entry problems.

Classroom doors are not locked during the school day; however, each has been equipped with a simple doorknob/lock combination (such as those found in many homes) so the doors can be locked from the inside with a turn of the wrist. The pane of glass nearest the doorknob has been replaced with a piece of wood to make it more difficult for an intruder to reach the lock by breaking the glass.

Volunteers (parents, grandparents, and senior citizens from the neighborhood) monitor the three instructional hallways each day. Monitor stations provide visual surveillance of the main hall and the three wings of the building. The monitor at the main lobby area directs all visitors into the office.

Visitors must wear conspicuous visitor badges. District office staff who visit the school must wear their identification badges at all times.

All custodians carry walkie-talkies for communication with the office. They report all activity that is out of the ordinary. At least one of the teachers who take classes to the playground area carries a walkie-talkie. The principal takes a walkie-talkie whenever she walks through the building.

Staff inservice activities provide information about access and evacuation of the building. These activities include controlled evacuation (as in a fire drill situation) and uncontrolled evacuation (when panic cannot be averted).

Student activities include instructions and practice in evacuating the building through doors and in evacuating the building through windows. These activities include tornado drills, fire drills, crash drills, intruder drills, and other drills that are specific to the school and campus. Students are also instructed about evacuating the playground area (into the building or into the neighborhood) in case of an intruder or other emergency.

Before school starts each year, the school invites all parents to visit the school. Part of that visit is a meeting in which early dismissal procedures are discussed in detail. Parents are told that they must come to the office to pick up a student before the end of the school day. A member of the office staff will go to the child's classroom to get the child. Under no circumstances will a teacher release a child to anyone except school staff. These procedures are outlined in a handbook given to each child on the first day of school and in a short letter mailed to each parent during the first week of school.

Also, before school starts each year, the school sponsors a neighborhood meeting, inviting all neighbors of the school, the police, the fire department, the rescue squad, representatives of industry and the airport, ministers from the local churches, and others who are interested. The safety of children is discussed. Specifically, the school safety and emergency plan is discussed and recommendations are taken.

The school also outlines procedures for gathering and sheltering who must be evacuated from the campus. Neighbors are given instructions about taking the children into their homes, getting lists of names, notifying school officials and local police of the situation, and othe procedures to ensure the safety of the children and themselves. The school mails a set of procedures to everyone who lives in the neighborhood.

Assigned Roles

Principal: The principal will coordinate and supervise emergency management activities at the school until intervention by the superintendent or other designated district staff. When district staff have begun the management process, the principal will supervise specific activities relating to the needs of the school, staff, students, and others involved in the emergency.

Assistant Principal: The assistant principal will act as the principal in the absence of the principal. The assistant principal will supervise and assist in specific activities relating to the needs of the school, staff, students, and others involved in the emergency. The assistant principal will supervise staff who have pre-defined roles (including substitute teachers, food service workers, volunteers, and others).

Guidance Counselor: The guidance counselor will be hired in the chain of command and communication. He or she will act as the assistant principal when the assistant principal is absent. The guidance counselor will supervise the immediate care of persons who are injured or hysterical, will assist in re-locating students to safe areas of the building or campus, will act as the intermediary for teachers and the school administrators. The guidance counselor will lead the efforts to identify injured students or staff.

Secretary and Office Aides: The principal's secretary and office aides will assist the guidance counselor in caring for injured or hysterical students and staff. If needed, the secretary will operate the computer system to obtain student and staff information.

Attendance Clerk: The attendance clerk will operate the personal computer and will answer the telephone during the emergency.

Custodians: All custodial staff will report immediately to the assistant principal to assist with traffic management and other duties. In the event of an evacuation, the custodial staff will check all classrooms to be sure that no one has been left in the building. If time permits, they will close all classroom windows and doors.

Food Service Staff: All food service staff will report immediately to the assistant principal. If food and shelter are needed, the food service staff will assist in planning and preparation.

Teachers and Classroom Aides: All teachers and classroom aides are to remain with their students at all times. The teacher should keep a class roster and should check it periodically to be sure all students are accounted for. Teachers will lead their students to safety based on the emergency procedures in the emergency plan. The materials taken with the teacher should identify persons who have permission to pick up students. The teacher should not release students to anyone who does not have specific permission to get the child.

Librarian and Other Staff: All remaining staff who do not have responsibility for students at the time of the emergency should report to the principal for duty assignments.

NOTE: If a staff member has specialized skills, such as CPR training, special plans should permit a teacher without direct responsibilities for students to relieve that teacher. That teacher should then report to any area where these specialized skills can be helpful.

ALARM SIGNALS

All students and personnel will be familiar with the alarm signals used for specific purposes. Drills and practice will be used to teach the alarms and the appropriate responses to these alarms.

Fire: A continuous ringing of the bell will signal immediate evacuation of the building, using the posted routes from each building area.

Bomb or bomb threat: A continuous ringing of the bell will signal immediate evactuation of the building, using the posted routes from each building area (same process as for fire).

Tornado: Short, intermittent ringing of the bell will signal that tornado procedures are to be followed.

Earthquake: A continuous ringing of the bell will signal immediate evacuation of the building, using the posted routes from each building area (same process as for fire).

Special alert: Short, intermittent ringing of the bell, accompanied by the continuous sound of the outside siren, will signal that special alert procedures are to be followed.

Voice and Hand Signals

All students and personnel will be familiar with the voice and hand signals used for specific purposes. Voice and hand signals may be particularly useful when an emergency occurs while students are outside the building. Drills and practice will be used to teach the signals and the appropriate responses to those signals.

Shout: When appropriate, a shout can be used to get the attention of the students. If a bullborn is available, it should be used.

When shouting or other voice signals are not appropriate or might endanger students, the following hand signals should be used:

Waving arms: Waving arms back and forth over the head means to follow. The students will follow in the direction lead by the teacher.

Palms down: Moving arms up and down with palms toward the

ground will signal the students to get down to the ground wherever they are at that time.

Palms out: Pushing palms out, moving arms forward and back, will signal the students to stop where they are and to stand absolutely still.

Waving arms side-to-side: Moving arms side-to-side in front of the body will signal the students to move away from the center of of the playground and to take shelter toward the edges of the playground.

NOTE: Procedures for each of the signals listed here are given in the Emergency Procedures section of this plan.

Emergency Procedures

Although every possible emergency cannot be anticipated, an attempt has been made to standardize emergency procedures and responses as much as possible.

Specific emergencies that might affect Kidville School include the following:

Accident or Serious Injury

1. When a student is seriously injured, the parents or guardians must be notified immediately.

2. First aid should be administered and the student comforted. A determination must be made regarding the severity of the injury and transportation to the hospital.

3. The emergency medical services should be called if the injury is serious enough to warrant special transportation. If the injury requires treatment but is not serious enough to warrant an ambulance, the principal or his or her designee may transport the student to the hospital (instead of waiting for the parents to come to the school).

4. The district must be notified of the injury.

Fire

1. When a fire is seen, the nearest fire alarm should be activated. This is done by pulling a lever on the fire alarm switch.

2. When a fire alarm is heard, each teacher will activate the evacuation procedure, which had been practiced in each class. That procedure ensures that all windows are closed and that students make an orderly exit from the classroom. The last person out of the classroom will close the classroom door.

3. Students and teachers exit the building through the designated doors. If the primary evacuation route is blocked by fire, alternate routes are taken.

4. When outside the building, each class moves quickly to a designated location on campus or to a designated location near the campus. The teacher must maintain control over the students for which he or she has responsibility.

5. The school secretary will call the local fire department or other emergency agencies.

6. The custodial staff will go directly to entrances to the campus and will direct all non-emergency traffic away from the building.

7. The principal will monitor the situation and will make decisions about moving groups of students away from areas that might be dangerous.

Bomb or Bomb Threat

1. When a bomb is seen or a bomb threat is received, the nearest fire alarm should be activated. This is done by pulling a lever on the fire alarm switch.

2. When a fire alarm is heard, each teacher will activate the evacuation procedure, which has been practiced in each class. This procedure ensures that all windows are closed and that students make an orderly exit from the classroom. The last person out of the classroom will close the classroom door.

3. Students and teachers exit the building through the designated doors. If the primary evacuation route is blocked, or if it is known that a bomb is in that particular area, alternate routes are taken.

4. When outside the building, each class moves quickly to a designated location on campus or to a designated location near the campus. The teacher must maintain control over the students for which he or she has responsibility.

5. The school secretary will call the local fire department or other emergency agencies.

6. The custodial staff will go directly to entrances to the campus and will direct all non-emergency traffic away from the building.

7. The principal will monitor the situation and will make decisions about moving groups of students away from areas that might be dangerous.

Tornado or High Winds

1. When a tornado warning is issued, when community warning

sirens are activated, or when a tornado is sighted, the tornado alarm will be sounded in the school building.

2. Custodial staff will report to assigned stations that will permit sight of weather conditions. They will report, directly to the principal, all threatening conditions.

3. All students, teachers, and other school staff will move into the hallways and other designated areas. Teachers must take class rosters or roll books with them.

4. All persons will assume the tornado preparation position. Teachers will observe their students to be sure they are in the proper position at all times.

Explosion

1. When an explosion occurs and debris is scattered in a classroom, students and teachers should immediately crawl under their desk tops. Eyes should be held tightly closed and arms should be used to cover heads. If time permits, jackets or books or other objects should be used to cover the head.

2. When the initial explosion has ended, teachers and students should evacuate the building, following normal evacuation routes. If normal routes are blocked, alternate routes (including windows) should be used.

3. When outside the building, each class moves quickly to a designated location on campus or to a designated location near the campus. The teacher must maintain control over the students for which he or she has responsibility.

4. The school secretary will call the local fire department or other emergency agencies.

5. The custodial staff will go directly to entrances to the campus and will direct all non-emergency traffic away from the building.

6. The principal will monitor the situation and will make decisions about moving groups of students away from areas that might be dangerous.

Intruder or Irrational Student or Staff

1. Parents and other volunteers monitor all halls in the building all during the school day. If a stranger enters the hallway, the monitor in that hallway will call to or signal another monitor who is nearer the office area. The second monitor will immediately go to the office to get help.

2. The monitor who sees the stranger will call to that stranger and will ask him or her to come directly to the office area. If the

stranger does not respond or acts in a strange manner, the monitor will continue to observe the stranger while calling loudly for assistance.

3. When teachers hear the monitor calling for assistance, they should immediately close and lock the classroom door. Under no circumstance is the teacher to leave the students.

4. Using a book or other hard object, the teacher will bang three times on the north and south walls of his or her classroom. That will be a signal to the next teacher that an intruder is in the hall and doors should be locked from the inside.

5. The teacher should warn the students of the possibility of some danger and should ask that they move to the floor under their desk tops. The teacher should also explain evacuation through the window in case it is needed.

6. The teacher should move to a safe place near the locked door and should do whatever is necessary to keep the intruder out of the classroom. That may mean that the teacher must use a hard object (textbook, yardstick, etc.) to hit at any hand that tries to come through the window to unlock the door.

7. The monitor at the end of the hall observes from a safe vantage point and keeps track of the intruder's movements. The monitor must know into which classroom the intruder has gone if the intruder is no longer in the hallway.

8. The office staff initiates a call to the police while the principal or his or her designee moves to the area where the intruder was observed.

9. The other monitors begin moving through their hallways, asking teachers to close and lock the classroom doors.

10. The office staff call custodians on their walkie-talkies and instruct them to move to the area where the intruder was observed.

11. Office staff also notify, by walkie-talkie, all teachers with students on the playground. These students are moved to the perimeter of the playground, away from the area where the intruder was observed.

12. As long as the intruder does not physically endanger students or staff, he or she is simply observed until law enforcement agents arrive. If students or staff are endangered, the principal, the monitor, and the custodial staff should do whatever is necessary to draw the attention of the intruder away from those students and staff members.

Incapacitated Teacher

1. If a teacher becomes incapacitated, one or more students should go immediately to the nearest classroom with a teacher and should tell that teacher of the problem. That teacher should go immediately to the aid of the incapacitated teacher.

2. A different student should go immediately to the office and should tell the secretary and principal. Someone from the office should go immediately to the classroom.

3. The secretary should place a call to an emergency medical services unit.

Attack on a Student or Staff Member

1. If a student or staff member is attacked in the building, students should know to leave the scene immediately and to seek help from the nearest teachers or from the office.

2. In the event of an attack on a student or staff member, other staff who witness the attack should do everything possible to distract the assailant — short of risking bodily harm.

3. The office will immediately notify the police and other agencies that can assist with the problem.

Bus Accident (Regular Route)

1. When the report of a bus accident comes in, the principal will print or have printed a list of students who normally ride that bus. That information will come from the computer records for the school. The list should include special medical considerations and signed medical releases provided by parents at the beginning of the school year (if any).

2. The principal or his or her designee will notify the superintendent and the supervisor of transportation for the district. (In most cases, these persons will already know because law enforcement officials will have contacted them.)

3. With the school emergency kit, the principal will go directly to the site of the accident.

4. The principal will assist in the identification of injured students.

5. If needed, the principal will provide a meeting location in the school for parents and school/district personnel.

Bus Accident (Field Trip)

1. Before a bus or buses leave with students going on a field trip, a list of riders for each bus will be left at the school. Riders are

expected to return on the same bus. A copy of the list is taken by one of the chaperons. A map of the routes to and from the field trip destination will be left at the school and will be clearly marked to show the routes.

2. When the report of the bus accident comes in, the principal or his or her designee will notify the superintendent and the supervisor of transportation for the district. (In most cases, these persons will already know because law enforcement officials will have contacted them.)

3. The principal will use the rider list to notify parents. If the location or condition of students is known, that information will be conveyed to the parents.

4. The principal will remain at the school while district and school staff go directly to the site of the accident and to hospital locations. Those who go to remote sites will carry a copy of the rider lists with them. (These are picked up at the school before leaving to go to the site.)

5. The attendance clerk will operate the computer and will print information from the records of students involved in the accident. The information will include medical considerations that can be relayed to hospitals serving the students and staff involved in the accident.

6. The principal, with the superintendent, will travel to the site of the accident and to the hospitals where victims are being treated.

Airplane Crash On or Near Campus

1. When an airplane crash occurs and the impact scatters debris into a classroom, students and teachers should immediately crawl under their desk tops. Eyes should be held tightly closed and arms should be used to cover heads. If time permits, jackets or books or other objects should be used to cover the head.

2. When the initial phase of the crash (which might include one or more explosions) has ended, teachers and students should evacuate the building, following normal evacuation routes. If normal routes are blocked, alternate routes (including windows) should be used.

3. When outside the building, each class moves quickly to a designated location on campus or to a designated location near the campus. The teacher must maintain control over the students for which he or she has responsibility.

4. The school secretary will call the local fire department or other emergency agencies.

5. The custodial staff will go directly to entrances to the campus and will direct all non-emergency traffic away from the building.

6. The principal will monitor the situation and will make decisions about moving groups of students away from areas that might be dangerous.

Emergency at Near-By Industry

1. If there is an explosion or chemical spill at a near-by industry, students should remain in the building. Students who are on the playground should be taken inside as soon as possible.

2. If the explosion or chemical spill is an immediate danger to the students and staff of the school — as indicated by mandates from the emergency preparedness agencies — students and staff should exit the building through the doors on the side of the building opposite the industry site. Standard fire drill routines will be in effect, except for the change in exit doors. In controlled lines, the students and staff should walk into the community and away from the industry site. Handicapped and other students who cannot walk will be placed in teachers' cars and driven to the district office.

3. The district will send buses to the school or to the evacuation route to pick up these children as they move and will take these children to a safe site.

Kidnapping or Hostage-Taking

1. If a student is kidnapped or taken hostage, the appropriate agencies must be notified immediately.

2. Witnesses to the kidnapping or hostage-taking should make every effort to get a description of the person or persons involved, should make every effort to identify the car or other means of escape, and should try to get the license number of the vehicle.

3. Witnesses should note the direction in which the persons leave campus.

The Emergency Kit

The following items are listed as a basis for creating and maintaining an Emergency Management Kit for Kidville School. The list includes specific items that may save time in implementing a school plan to manage emergencies. Additional items may be needed and can be added to the kit.

[ ] 20 legal pads (8½" × 11" and 4" × 5")

[ ] 20 ballpoint pens (not felt-tip and not pencils)

[ ] 20 Magic Markers

[ ] 500 plain white peel-off stickers (to be used to identify injured students or adults at the emergency site)

[ ] List of telephone numbers for the district office, local law enforcement agencies, emergency medical services, fire department, and other agencies that may need to know of a school crisis

[ ] List of telephone numbers for the cellular telephones used by district staff

[ ] List of computer, BBS, and fax lines at the district office

[ ] List of beeper numbers for district staff

[ ] 1 local telephone directory

[ ] 1 current staff directory for district

[ ] Floor plan that shows the location of all exits, all telephones and telephone wall jacks, computer locations, and all other devices that may be useful in communication during an emergency

[ ] 1 fully charged battery-operated bullhorn

[ ] Local street and zone maps

[ ] For all off-campus trips, a map showing the route to be traveled to and from the off-campus destination

[ ] For all off-campus trips, a list of students and adults on each bus or vehicle should be left at the school; students and adults must ride the same bus both ways

[ ] List of assigned roles for school personnel and district personnel

[ ] Recent lists of students who ride buses, given by bus/route number

[ ] Summary of information that can be made public during an emergency; include Freedom of Information summary, district policy, and others

[ ] List of professional and community contacts for organizing a "crisis care team" of counselors, ministers, and others

[ ] Teacher packets, including student lists, paper, pens, pencils, etc.

[ ] Medical emergency list, including names of students with special medical considerations

[ ] First aid manual

OTHER CONSIDERATIONS

Kidville School understands that early dismissal of schools, whether for an emergency or for weather (snow and ice storms), can put some children at risk. In some cases, there may be no adult at home when the child arrives there. In an effort to remedy these situations, the school and the district will provide announcements of early dismissals to local radio and television stations. When parents hear of an emergency or see that weather may be a factor, they should make immediate arrangements to provide supervision for all children who may be sent home.

In special cases in which the parents feels that he or she will not hear the announcements, he or she may request individual notification of early dismissal. The school will make every effort to telephone such parents.

Although there are only two published telephone numbers for the school, the telephone company has placed a box in the office area from which six additional lines can be run, if needed.

Training

Staff and students will be trained in carrying out the emergency activities described in this emergency plan. These training sessions will be completed during the first week of school and will be reinforced near the beginning of the second semester.

Review and Revision

This emergency plan will be reviewed prior to the start of each school year and near the beginning of the second semester. The review will be made to determine the need for revisions based on changing situations, staff, or resources.

Conclusions

The safety and well-being of the students at Kidville School is of prime importance. This emergency plan is designed to provide guidance in the handling of students as emergencies occur. When necessary, good judgment may dictate that parts of this plan be changed as an emergency unfolds. Such changes will always be made with the safety of students in mind.

APPENDIX B

A Sample District Emergency Plan

THIS APPENDIX includes sample emergency plans for the district level. These plans include communications, assigned roles of staff, dealing with the media, transportation, and other activities that require district intervention. The sample district plans have been developed from the procedures described in Chapter 11. The development process is outlined, as well.

STEPS FOR DEVELOPING THE DISTRICT OFFICE EMERGENCY PLAN

I. Meet with district office staff to analyze resources
   1. Review geographic locations of schools
   2. Assess personnel capabilities
   3. Review current board policy and procedures regarding emergencies
   4. Review types of emergencies that might occur
   5. Assess community resources available to the district
   6. Assess school district communications capabilities (including available technology)
   7. Review all available school emergency plans
II. Develop an emergency plan
   1. Assign emergency roles for all available personnel
   2. Develop emergency communications plan with specified technology
   3. Develop district emergency kit
   4. Supervise the development of school emergency plans
   5. Install necessary safety devices and develop necessary procedures
   6. Provide staff development training for district staff and principals

III. Coordinate district plan with school and community plans
   1. Seek input from schools regarding district plan components
   2. Seek input from local emergency personnel and agencies
   3. Coordinate district plan with all local emergency plans (police, fire, emergency/rescue, etc.)
IV. Inform all school and community publics of the plan
   1. Publish the plan and disseminate adequate number of copies
   2. Develop ready-reference format for district and school employees
V. Train all taff and volunteer personnel
   1. Include all members of faculty and staff
   2. Plan and implement a mock disaster
VI. Share plan with interested state and local agencies as requested

Introduction to the District Plan

Seldom is an organization prepared for sudden, potentially destructive events. Schools have always been vulnerable to disaster because large numbers of people are collected in relatively small spaces. As a result, natural disasters, accidents, and intentional intrusions that involve schools can have devastating effects on students, staff, parents, and the community as a whole. Schools can be the objects of vicious attacks by armed persons or caught up in the spill-over effects of turbulent community unrest.

The vulnerability of schools may be found in their essential openness. That openness is a condition of life in a democratic and open public school system that reflects the society in which it serves. It is necessary, however, to have contingency plans available to enact quick, effective responses to minimize the disastrous effects that certain types of calamities can bring.

Communications

The district will use all available technology for the gathering and dissemination of information during a school emergency. That process requires an effective communication system, involving available hardware, software, and staff trained to manage these.

The primary objective for establishing effective communication during an emergency is to collect all information relevant to the persons and events involved in the emergency and to disseminate all appropriate information to parents, families, law enforcement agencies, medical service agencies, print and electronic media representatives, the general community, and others. By effectively managing communication, the district can provide necessary services to its students and staff and to the families of these persons. In addition, the effective dissemination of information will counter problems caused by unfounded rumors.

Each school in the district will be prepared for effective communication when an emergency occurs. The following items will be placed in each school for such purposes:

1. At least two telephone lines with unpublished numbers
2. At least one telephone line with an unpublished number
3. At least one data line attached via modem to the school computer
4. All RJ-11 jacks for telephone and computer lines
5. All wall jacks located and marked with wall stickers
6. A strong recommendation that telephone systems be upgraded to stay active when power is out
7. At least one cellular telephone
8. Walkie-talkies for the principal, assistant principal, and other staff who patrol the buildings and grounds (such as custodians)
9. Walkie-talkies for teachers who have classes on remote areas of the campus (such as physical education classes)
10. A bullhorn that recharges its batteries when not in use
11. Computer access to the district electronic bulletin board system (via modem)
12. Intercom systems with teacher-initiated call capabilities from each classroom
13. Some schools will have a "panic button" directly connected to the law enforcement agencies
14. An emergency communication kit that will contain an abundant supply of batteries (all appropriate sizes), telephone line with RJ-11 connectors on each end, a list of all district telephone numbers, BBS numbers, fax numbers, and others
15. A current backup copy of all student computer files (on diskette format that can be loaded immediately into a portable computer)

In the event of a school emergency, the district will provide additional communication capabilities. When district staff arrive at the school, they will bring a portable facsimile machine (fax), a portable computer with modem, cellular telephones, and walkie-talkies. Other communication devices may also be provided by district staff.

Two important communication capabilities will be provided by the district:

1. A district staff member will go directly to the Emergency Preparedness Center at the county courthouse and will assist in communicating with law enforcement agencies, medical services agencies, and other agencies that may be able to help meet the needs of those involved in the emergency.

2. The district will maintain a multi-line electronic bulletin board system (BBS) through which schools can access the district office and other schools. In addition, in an emergency, law enforcement agencies and emergency services agencies will be given access to the BBS so that they can monitor events and offer help when needed. In addition, the BBS can be used (from a portable computer at a remote location) to send the names and conditions of students or adults involved in an emergency away from the school campus.

When an emergency occurs, the Director of Computing Services, the Computer Technician, and the Secretary in the Office of Computing Services will begin the process of monitoring the communication needs during the emergency. When there is a breakdown in communication, one or more of that team will respond and will make every effort to correct the problem.

Training

It is important that all school and district staff know their responsibilities during a school emergency. It is, therefore, necessary to provide training to all staff members.

Principals will provide training to all school staff, including all instructional, custodial, and food service employees. The training should be based on the school emergency/safety plans. The best time for training is at the beginning of each school year, with appropriate practice for such procedures as evacuating students, manning emergency stations, locking doors, etc. Each school emergency plan should include staff training procedures. These procedures ought to provide for an annual review and approval of the plan by the School Improvement Council.

District training will include an annual review of the district plan and an annual training session or sessions to include the principals and all district office staff. That training will take place during the summer administrators' workshops or during inservice days prior to the beginning of school each year.

Training for the district plan will be coordinated with the local police and fire departments and with all local emergency preparedness agencies. District training will include all components of the district plan, including (1) the assigned roles of all district staff, (2) use of emergency kits and equipment, (3) the role of the media, and (4) updating of communication plans. Other items will be added to that agenda as needed.

The Media

I. Philosophy

The district provides access to all public information through cooperative efforts among representatives of the media and district personnel while considering the responsibilities of both agencies.

The primary objective for effective media utilization is to inform the public of all relevant information during a district/school emergency.

II. Regulations
   1. The Director of Teacher and Community Services will be the designated person to work with the media. All media requests will be directed through him or her.
   2. At no time will students be interviewed without parental approval. When requests for student interviews are granted, the interview will be completed with minimum loss of instructional time, minimum interruption in the learning environment, and approval from the Superintendent's office.
   3. Teachers and other employees are free to grant interviews with the media when the interview will not interrupt the employee's responsibilities. (The Director of Teacher and Community Services should be informed of all interviews, if possible.)
   4. The school or district will assign a location for the media which is convenient for them and which will meet the requirements of both the media and school personnel.
   5. As soon after an emergency as is reasonably possible, the Chairman of the Board of Trustees, the Superintendent, the Director of Teacher and Community Services, and

others will meet to establish relevant position statements on topics about which the media will have questions.
6. The Director of Teacher and Community Services will prepare notes for speakers involved in news conferences and will prepare written statements for the press.
7. The Director of Teacher and Community Services will prepare and distribute a fact sheet which contains relevant information about students and personnel and about the population, location, history, etc. of the emergency site.
8. The Director of Teacher and Community Services will provide the media personnel with media guidelines established by the school district.

III. Internal Communication Network

The Director of Teacher and Community Services will keep district employees updated frequently. This will be accomplished through the district BBS. The BBS will be accessed by modem through the laptop computer from the Office of Teacher and Community Services.

IV. Media Contacts

The district maintains a listing of all local newspapers, radio stations, and television stations. A list of all statewide newspapers, radio stations, and television stations is also maintained. Both lists contain the names of contact persons, telephone numbers, and fax numbers. When an emergency occurs, these contacts are notified and plans begin to accommodate their need to gather information about the emergency. The lists are attached.

V. Key Communicators

The district maintains a listing of prominent persons and community leaders on whom it can rely to provide assistance and to help disseminate information. These persons are contacted as soon as possible after the emergency occurs.

VI. Local Cable Channel Access

The district works with the local cable television company to have 24-hour access to a cable channel. The district broadcasts on Cable Channel 01, which displays a "scroll" of information for cable viewers.

During the initial crisis, a member of the ETV staff will report to the scene at the request of the Director of Teacher and Community Services. The ETV Technician will then collect relevant footage for broadcasting and will record all news conferences. He or she will report directly to the Director of Teacher and Community Services for assignment.

One ETV Technician will remain at the studio and prepare for immediate broadcasting on Channel 01 which will involve removing the scroll and placing emergency announcements on the channel.

After adequate footage is obtained at the scene of the emergency, Channel 01 will begin full, continuous coverage with spokespersons being assigned for taping frequent updates.

VII. Media Emergency Kits
1. Copy of district/school emergency plan
2. Lists of all media contacts
3. Name tags for media personnel
4. Copy of Freedom of Information regulations

Transportation

I. Introduction

During an emergency, students, parents, and administrators may need to move from one location to another. For example, students may have to be evacuated from a school very rapidly. Administrators or parents may need to travel great distances to meet with injured or stranded students in some remote location. School buses may be needed at unusual hours. Bus drivers may have to be summoned quickly and dispatched to a school to take students home.

II. Regulations
1. The Assistant Superintendent for Administration will supervise all transportation. He or she will coordinate and direct transportation services for injured persons and members of their families.
2. No student will be released to any adult without authorization from an administrator. Upon direction from the supervising administrator, arrangements will be made for the safe dismissal of all students.
3. The decision to transport students in other than authorized school vehicles will be made by the Assistant Superintendent for Administration.
4. Each school will designate a safe holding area, which is located in close proximity to the school, for students to

wait for the arrival of buses or parents. This area will be kept free of vehicle traffic.
   5. The district will include bus drivers in their annual training activities.
III. Bus Emergency Kit
Each bus in the district will carry an emergency kit which contains the following:
   Pencils
   Paper
   Stick-on name tags
   Phone number list
   Student roster
   First aid kit
   Signs to display bus numbers
   Area maps
   Route maps
IV. Emergency Telephone Numbers
Telephone numbers for emergency medical services, police, the district office, the highway patrol, the local hospital, and for beepers worn by district staff will be listed in this plan.

Roles of Selected District Office Staff in a School Emergency

The district specifies and assigns activities and tasks to each district-level employee. These are to be fulfilled in any school emergency. A chain of command is in place, and a chain of substitution is included for use when certain members of the emergency management team are not available during a school emergency.

The Superintendent

Direct all operations of the district in the management of the emergency.

Gather information from all aspects of the emergency for use in in making appropriate decisions about the management of the emergency.

Assess the emergency situation and assign tasks based on the overall needs of managing the emergency.

Direct all activities of district and school staff in the management of the emergency.

Stay in contact with the leaders of the emergency service agencies and the law enforcement agencies working with the emergency.

Authorize the release of information to the public.

The Assistant Superintendent for Instruction

Coordinate and direct persons with predefined assignments.

Establish and implement plans for crisis care; form and coordinate crisis-care teams.

Maintain active file of helping agencies within the community; the names of contact persons will be included.

Maintain active file of community persons, such as counselors, doctors, psychologists, ministers; information regarding services and follow-up services will be included.

Create letters to notify parents of continuing care that is available to students; available care will include local and state agencies, as well as school-based care.

Develop information sheet for parents, teachers, and others; information will include topics such as talking with students, signs of depression, and others relating to crisis stress.

Assist with planning a community forum for follow-up activities.

Maintain and initiate contacts for inservice, insurance, workers' compensation, and other staff services.

Plan and initiate arrangements for food for building personnel.

Handle overflow telephone calls at the emergency site.

Receive dignitaries who come to help or gather information.

Confer with full staff and faculty; coordinate briefings for staff and faculty.

Plan and implement post-monthly meetings with staff, faculty, and administrators.

Make recommendations regarding the re-starting of school activities.

Develop schedule for activities for the first day of school following the crisis.

Maintain follow-up activities such as referrals for help outside the school services setting.

The Assistant Superintendent for Personnel

Set up the district command center at the school involved in the emergency.

Supervise the collection of information about those involved in the emergency.

Identify all injured and missing students and adults involved in the emergency.

Check student and staff records for all injured to determine special medical needs that may be on file.

Notify parents of students and spouses of staff who are involved in the emergency.

Supervise the emergency communications network.

Determine information to be disseminated based on the Freedom of Information Act and the Right to Privacy laws.

Supervise dissemination of information to media.

The Assistant Superintendent for Administration

Report immediately to the Emergency Preparedness Center at the county courthouse.

Serve as a liaison between the emergency school site and the emergency support teams that may be needed.

Coordinate and direct transportation services for injured persons, school students and staff, and parents.

Coordinate and direct communication between the emergency site and county and state agencies.

Obtain and direct the placement of generators when power must be restored for a temporary period.

Coordinate and direct the acquisition of water when there is a disruption of water and sewer services.

Coordinate and direct contact with emergency medical services, local police and sheriff's departments, fire departments, and the highway patrol.

Coordinate and direct search-and-rescue operations when needed.

The Assistant Superintendent for Business and Operations

From the district offices, direct all district office staff.

Establish and maintain lines of communication between the district and the emergency site; for off-campus emergency, lines of communication must be established for the involved school, as well. Such lines of communication may also include couriers.

Establish and maintain a clearing house for calls and requests from school, the community, parents, the media, etc. and refer these to the appropriate person or place.

Manage the professional and non-professional staff from the district office.

Assign resources (persons and materials) to various sites for specific needs.

Communicate with other schools in the district during the emergency period.

After other schools have closed, assign those principals to sites and tasks that will benefit the district's attempts to manage the emergency.

Arrange for the payment of monies needed to respond to emergency situations; authorize purchases and payments for such resources.

Arrange for the delivery of outside services and materials needed for the management of the emergency.

The Director of Teacher and Community Services

Collect and disseminate information to the media. Be aware of deadlines, the need for accuracy, and other issues related to the media and their performance of their jobs.

Plan and coordinate press conferences.

Create and disseminate press releases.

Respond to rumors through the dissemination of accurate information.

Organize a network of key people within the community through which accurate information can be disseminated.

Be aware of the requirements of the Freedom of Information Act and provide all appropriate information based on these requirements.

Plan and coordinate the use of the district's cable television channel for live and taped presentations. Press conferences can go out live; updates for the public can be taped and aired as needed.

Coordinate information to be shared with school and district personnel during and after the crisis.

Act as a buffer between the media and district personnel whose attention must be focused on the immediate problems of managing the crisis.

Arrange interviews for the media with key school and district staff who are involved in the emergency or who act as spokespersons for the district.

The Director of Secondary Education

Report immediately to the local hospital if students or adults are being sent to that hospital for treatment.

Report to remote hospitals to which students or adults have been admitted for treatment.

If more than one hospital is admitting students or adults, coordinate the communication among these hospitals and the district. Assign and direct other district staff to assist in these hospitals.

Coordinate communication between the hospital and the district office.

Meet and talk with the parents of students and the spouses of adults who have been admitted to the hospital.

Direct the Chapter 1 Coordinator to assist in any of the roles and tasks necessary to accomplish the above tasks.

The Director of Elementary Education

Report to the Assistant Superintendent for Business and Operations at the District Office.

Complete tasks assigned by the Assistant Superintendent for Business and Operations.

The Director of Computing Services

Plan and coordinate the upgrading of existing telephone systems in each school to accommodate a private line, computer interfaces, and the movement of handsets from one location to another.

Develop plans and scenarios in which district technological resources can be dispersed effectively to emergency sites.

Prepare and maintain an emergency kit that contains floor plans, telephone line locations, computer locations, and other communications equipment.

Report to the Assistant Superintendent for Personnel at the emergency site or at the school involved in an off-campus emergency.

Establish and maintain computer communication with the district office and other agencies capable of such communication.

Establish and maintain a stand-alone computer with student and staff database for use at the emergency site. Assist in obtaining needed student and staff information from the computer files.

Supervise the use of the school computer system for communication with the district office and electronic bulletin board system.

As needed, report to various sites involved in the communication system if there are problems in that system.

Provide technical support for all communications hardware and software.

Assist in other areas designated by the Assistant Superintendent for Personnel or other supervisor.

The Director of Special Services
Report to the Assistant Superintendent for Business and Operations at the District Office.
Assist the Assistant Superintendent for Instruction in implementing plans for crisis care and in forming and coordinating crisis care teams.
Under the supervision of the Assistant Superintendent for Instruction, direct the involvement of the Psychological Services staff in the crisis-care effort.

The Director of Adult Education
Report to the Assistant Superintendent for Business and Operations at the District Office.
Complete tasks assigned by the Assistant Superintendent for Business and Operations.
Complete specific tasks assigned by the Assistant Superintendent for Instruction.

The Coordinator of ETV Services
Report immediately to the Director of Teacher and Community Services at the school involved in the crisis.
Videotape all news conferences and prepare the videotapes for broadcast over the district cable channel.
Coordinate the videotaping of specific events and the broadcasting of these tapes through regular or special ETV channels.

The Staff Development Coordinator
Report to the Assistant Superintendent for Business and Operations at the District Office.
Complete tasks assigned by the Assistant Superintendent for Business and Operations.

The EIA Coordinator
Report to the Assistant Superintendent for Business and Operations at the District Office.
Complete tasks assigned by the Assistant Superintendent for Business and Operations.

The Chapter 1 Coordinator

Report to the Director of Secondary Education and act under his or her direction in the following locations.

Report immediately to the local hospital if students or adults are being sent to that hospital for treatment.

Report to remote hospitals to which students or adults have been admitted for treatment.

The Reading/Language Arts Coordinator

Report to the Assistant Superintendent for Business and Operations at the District Office.

Complete tasks assigned by the Assistant Superintendent for Business and Operations.

The Teacher Evaluation Coordinator

Report to the Assistant Superintendent for Business and Operations at the District Office.

Complete tasks assigned by the Assistant Superintendent for Business and Operations.

The Computer Technician

Report to the Assistant Superintendent for Personnel at the school involved in the emergency.

Operate the school's computer in the search for student and adult information.

Operate the school's computer in the communication with the District Office and with other agencies.

Assist the Director of Computing Services in the maintenance of communications and software at the school site.

The Secretary to the Director of Computing Services

Report to the Assistant Superintendent for Business and Operations at the District Office.

Monitor and operate the district's electronic bulletin board system.

Provide frequent updates of information to the Assistant Superintendent for Business and Operations.

Place appropriate information on the electronic bulletin board system for dissemination to the emergency site, to other schools, to the county Emergency Preparedness Center, and to other agencies using the BBS.

Secretaries, Clerks, Warehouse Employees and
Other Support Staff

Report to the Assistant Superintendent for Business and Operations at the District Office.

Complete tasks assigned by the Assistant Superintendent for Business and Operations.

Principals

Remain at respective schools until the end of the school day.

When all students and staff members have left campus for the day, report to the Assistant Superintendent for Business and Operations at the District Office.

Perform tasks assigned by the Assistant Superintendent for Business and Operations.

ABOUT THE AUTHORS

Robert S. Watson, Ph.D.
Dr. Watson was Superintendent of Greenwood School District 50, Greenwood, South Carolina, during the time of a bus accident involving 47 students and teachers. Also during his tenure at Greenwood, there was an incident in which eleven students and teachers were shot, two fatally. Since 1989, he has been Superintendent of Traverse City Area Public Schools in Michigan.

Janice H. Poda, Ph.D.
Dr. Poda was Assistant Superintendent for Personnel in Greenwood School District during the bus accident and shooting incident. She is now the Director of the Teacher Recruitment Center for the State of South Carolina.

C. Thomas Miller, Ed.D.
Dr. Miller was Director of Teacher and Community Services for Greenwood School District during the bus accident and shooting incident. He is now the principal of Southside Junior High School in Greenwood, South Carolina.

Eleanor S. Rice
Ms. Rice is the principal of Oakland Elementary School in Greenwood, South Carolina. She was the principal, in 1988, when an intruder shot eleven students and teachers, killing two third-graders.

Gary West
Mr. West is the Director of Computing Service for Greenwood School District 50.

DO YOU HAVE AN IDEA TO SHARE?

The National Educational Service is always looking for high-quality manuscripts that have practical application for educators and others who work with youth.

Do you have a new, innovative, or especially effective approach to some timely issue? Does one of your colleagues have something burning to say on curriculum development, professionalism in education, excellence in teaching, or some other aspect of education? If so, we would love to hear from you. Please contact Nancy Shin, Director of Publications.

Containing Crisis: A Guide to Managing School Emergencies is one of the many publications produced by the National Educational Service. Our mission is to provide you and other leaders in education, business, and government with timely, top-quality publications, videos, and conferences. We also provide in-service training and professional development on a variety of topics including:

Discipline with Dignity
Reclaiming Youth at Risk
Cooperative Learning
Thinking Across the Curriculum
Cooperative Management
Parental Involvement

If you have any questions or comments about *Containing Crisis,* or if you want more information on our professional development services, contact us at:

National Educational Service
1610 West Third Street
P.O. Box 8
Bloomington, IN 47402
1-800-733-6786
1-812-336-7700
1-812-336-7790 (FAX)

NEED MORE COPIES?

Need more copies of this book? Want your own copy? If so, you can order additional copies of *Containing Crisis: A Guide to Managing School Emergencies,* by using this form or by calling us at (800) 733-6786 (US only) or (812) 336-7700. Or you can order by FAX at (812) 336-7790.

We guarantee complete satisfaction with all of our materials. If you are not completely satisfied with any NES publication, you may return it to us within 30 days for a full refund.

	Quantity	Total
Containing Crisis: A Guide to Managing School Emergencies ($19.95 each)	_____	_____
Shipping: Add $2.00 per copy		_____
(There is no shipping charge when you ***include*** payment with your order)		
Indiana residents add 5% sales tax		_____
	TOTAL	_____

❏ Check enclosed with order   ❏ Please bill me
❏ VISA, MasterCard, or Discover   ❏ Money order
❏ P.O.#_____

Account No._____ Exp. Date _____
Cardholder _____
Ship to:
Name_____ Title _____
Organization _____
Address _____
City_____ State_____ ZIP _____
Phone _____
Fax _____

MAIL TO:
National Educational Service
1610 W. Third Street
P.O. Box 8
Bloomington, IN 47402